UNDERCOVER IN THE JUNGLE

UNDERCOVER IN THE JUNGLE

John Bowen

WILLIAM KIMBER · LONDON

First published in 1978 by
WILLIAM KIMBER & CO. LIMITED
Godolphin House, 22a Queen Anne's Gate,
London, SW1H 9AE

© John Bowen, 1978
ISBN 0 7183 0226 5

Typeset by Jubal Multiwrite Ltd, London SE13
and printed in Great Britain
by Redwood Burn Limited, Trowbridge and Esher.

Contents

List of Maps

List of illustrations

For Elaine

Acknowledgements

I would like to acknowledge the work of my sister Elisabeth Leslie in preparing the maps, and the kind permission given to me thirty years ago by my friend Michael Fielding, journalist and broadcaster of Chicago, to use his photographs as illustrations.

Prologue

I believe that very few people are to any real extent masters of their fate, but that most of us have a great capacity for looking back on our past lives and explaining the medley of decisions that go to make them up in the light of a master plan that we come to believe that we were nursing in our minds from the very start.

Even at the present time I find myself having to exercise considerable self-control in order to resist the temptation to believe that everything that happened to me in Burma occurred in just the way I had intended. Writing in 1946 before the memory of it grows dim, I am convinced that it was entirely as a result of a series of chance incidents that I came to find myself serving in the organisation known as V Force and later as a parachutist with Force 136 in Karenni.

One day early in 1943 I was sitting in the rest camp at Maungdaw in the Arakan listening to the twenty-five pounders firing up on the Mayu Ridge. The battle was going against us and the Punjabi battalion which I was due to rejoin after my leave was cut off in the Kalapanzin Valley by a Japanese force astride the Maungdaw—Buthidaung road in the Tunnels area. Being in the battle area for the first time I was keen and enthusiastic and had offered to try to rejoin it by a circuitous route through the hills known as the Goppe Pass, but my suggestion had been turned down by the Camp Commandant as impractical.

Then towards evening a square thickset young captain wearing an MC ribbon on his tunic had for a moment entered the mess on some pretext or other. Someone had asked him where he was going and he had replied:

'Over the Goppe Pass.'

After he had gone I asked why he should be allowed to go by that route when I could not, and I was told that he was in a guerilla organisation called V Force, and that V Force officers worked alone. At that moment the work of a V Force Officer seemed romantic and exciting and infinitely more attractive than the infantry. But I was a company commander, and my battalion was short of officers and the thought of applying for a transfer never entered my head.

Nearly eighteen months later I was still in the Arakan. My battalion had taken some hard knocks but had finally won quite a name for itself on the West Finger feature south of the Maungdaw—Buthidaung road. It was due to be withdrawn to a peace station in India for a long rest. Of the old officers only three remained, and, for a variety of reasons, I was anxious for a change. At the same time the prospect of a staff job in India did not attract me. During the previous monsoon I had commanded a fighting patrol that had crossed the wild uninhabited mountains that lie between the Kalapanzin Valley and the Kaladan River to the remote little Pi Chaung in pursuit of an enemy guerilla force that, in fact, did not exist. It had been a very unsuccessful patrol, but during the course of it I had learned something of life in the jungle, and I had come to know a number of V Force officers personally. In May 1944 I wrote to one of these and asked him what prospects there were of my being taken into the formation. He replied that they were good, and told me to send in an application through my unit. With some trepidation I approached the Adjutant and rather to my surprise the Colonel wrote me out a suitable testimonial. In the fullness of time the transfer was effected and I was flown north into Imphal which was then being besieged by the largest Japanese force that had ever been put into the field at any one time.

PART ONE

Manipur

1

Imphal is the capital of Manipur, a little Indian native state in the Arabian Nights tradition. It is set in the midst of a rich rice plain surrounded on all sides by rugged mountain ranges. Being a border region, it is even in peacetime never quite at peace. A single motor road connects it via Kohima with Dimapur and the metre gauge railway into India proper. At the time of my arrival in June 1944 the British 2nd Division was pushing forward from railhead along this road against desperate Japanese resistance in an attempt to raise the siege. The besieged garrison was being supplied from the air by the RAF, who were competing against a rapidly approaching monsoon, and the troops were reduced to half-rations. Along most of the main tracks leading down from the mountains into the Imphal plain the Japanese were making a last desperate bid for victory.

East of Imphal there is a good mule track through Ukhrul to the Burma border in the Kabaw Valley and the Chindwin River beyond. Here the Japanese were being held by the Indian 20th Division which had an Indian parachute brigade in an ordinary infantry role working on its right flank. To the south there is a wild inaccessible mountain region where a V Force officer called Pip Fraser-Smith was commanding an isolated little guerilla force of Naga and Kuki tribesmen stiffened by a handful of men from the Assam Rifles, a military police battalion that kept order along the frontier in peace time. South of his area again there is another good mule track crossing the mountains from Imphal to the Chindwin through Palel and Tamu. Here the Indian 23rd Division was held up by a composite force of Japanese and traitor-Indians from the Japanese controlled Indian National Army.

I was ordered to join Pip Fraser-Smith. He came into Imphal for a conference soon after my arrival and together we travelled back to his headquarters in the little Naga village called Manwunjang.

Pip Fraser-Smith was a tall fair-haired young man of twenty-two with a very serious disposition for his age. He was charming, intelligent, and brave, and, if he had not been so very untidily dressed when I first met him, I should probably have thought him polished. When the enemy had first crossed the Chindwin he had been on a reconnaissance patrol on the east bank with a swashbuckling V Force Jemedar of mixed Indian and Kuki parentage called Mani Ram and a Gurkha from the Assam Rifles. Pip had swum the river in broad daylight under the noses of the Japs to steal a boat with which to get the others across. This having been safely accomplished, they had set off together on the long trek to Imphal. They had moved through country stiff with alert offensive Japanese troops and over a period of a month in the mountains they had been nearly always without food, but in the end they had regained the British lines. Pip had been awarded the MC and Mani Ram the IDSM. In spite of this arduous experience Pip had volunteered to return to the hills to re-open a guerilla area that had existed in Manwunjang before the invasion.

In the Imphal zone of V Force there had been two lieutenant-colonels' commands, 2 V Ops and 3 V Ops, each made up of three to four sub-areas. But by this time 2 V Ops and 3 V Ops had ceased to exist in the chaos of the Japanese advance on Imphal and the sub-area that Pip was operating was the only one that existed as such.

We travelled by truck as far as Yairipok and were provided with a fine meal by the Manipuri *kalackwa* (headman) of the village at the foot of the mountains. He was a fat jovial figure wearing a caste thread round his bare belly which he wriggled whenever Pip made a humorous remark. Thus fortified we set off up the hill into the mist carrying our rucksacks on our backs. It was very different country from the low fever-stricken Arakan. The air was cleaner and the vegetation less luxuriant and tropical, and the path rose steeply like an endless staircase. All the afternoon we zigzagged up the hillside into grey impenetrable cloud and I soon began to realise the extent of my unfitness. After the second hour I had to ask for a long rest. Pip was most sympathetic but he looked at me rather in the way that a school prefect looks at a small boy who has fallen out on a cross country run and I felt embarrassed. At about six o'clock we came to a village, where everyone seemed to know Pip, and halted for half an hour. The *kalackwa* brought us a great bowl of *zoo* (rice beer) which we drank through bamboo straws. It tasted not unlike cider and must have had a similar strength.

'These are Kukis,' remarked Pip as he sucked away at his straw. I looked about me and saw that the men wore dirty white woollen smocks that did not reach more than a few inches below their waists. Their hair was long and drawn into a bun at the back of their heads. They seemed naturally beardless and even the oldest of them had little more than thin straggling moustaches drooping from either side of their lips. Their faces were round and Mongolian and they regarded us with intelligent fearless eyes.

'They're mostly bastards,' Pip added so abstractedly that I looked surprised.

'The villages in these hills are either Kuki or Naga. The two peoples speak different languages, but they all understand the local *lingua franca*, which is Manipuri. The Kukis are in a way slightly more enterprising than the Nagas, but they are far less reliable. There was a Kuki rebellion after the last war when they led the Assam Rifles quite a dance and nowadays a lot of them are working for the Japs.'

'What about the Nagas?' I asked.

'They used to be headhunters, and still are a little further north beyond the Somra Frontier Tract in the Unadministered Territory. But down here they're peaceable enough. In fact they're a little too peaceloving for my taste. In the early days of V Force it was quite impossible to get them to come and work for us, and we had to rely entirely on the Kukis. But now the Nagas are the only ones we can really trust, and I think they'll come out and fight the Japs.'

When we had finished the *zoo* and resumed our trek, Pip took with us two Kuki porters to carry our rucksacks as far as the Naga village of Manwunjang which was about an hour's march away up the hill. Darkness had fallen before we arrived, but for some time I

could see fires gleaming on the mountainside in front. The last
stage was along a narrow knife-edge on either side of which the
hillside seemed to fall away into what looked like a bottomless pit
in the surrounding blackness. I saw it later in the daytime and it
was not nearly so terrifying as when I first saw it that night. My
calves were by then aching horribly. We had climbed three
thousand feet during the afternoon and the village of Manwunjang
was at the point where the track crossed the first range. Pip paid
off our coolies in the village and we scrambled on up the slope to
the V Force camp in the darkness carrying our own loads. I felt at
the end of my tether.

'Why the hell did you pay off those Kukis?' I asked.

'Because I don't want anyone to know too much about this
camp,' Pip replied. 'Especially not Kukis.' In the darkness in front
a voice rasped an Indianised version of 'Halt. Who goes there?' Pip
identified us and we moved into a little hut where three Gurkhas
from the Assam Rifles and a number of V Force scouts were
crouching round a fire. He spoke to them in Gurkhali which I did
not then understand. Apparently everything was to his satisfaction.

'This is only the guard post,' he explained. 'No one who I don't
trust implicitly is ever allowed past it. The rest of the camp is
about four hundred yards up the hill.'

Beyond the guard post we crossed a disused mountain paddy
field and then entered some undergrowth, through which I slipped
and slid in almost complete darkness with Pip urging me on rather
in the same way that a house prefect at school urges on a young
hope in the last lap of the junior mile. Then we reached the camp.
There were two huts with floors raised above the ground on which
to sleep. They were built of local trees and their roofs were
tarpaulins. Pip and I had a little cubicle at the end of the one

occupied by the twenty Assam Riflemen that he had with him.
The other was occupied by a duty party of Kukis and Nagas from
the neighbouring villages. But all that I learned the following day.
That night I felt almost too tired to eat the meal that Pip's orderly
set before us, but I felt happier than I had felt for a very long
time.

*

When I woke up the next morning the whole camp was swathed in mist, and a wet film of dew had formed over everything that had not been covered up the night before. Pip's orderly, looking like a little gnome with a cap-comforter pulled down about his ears, brought us both a mug of very sweet tea and a tin full of hot water with which to shave. When I climbed out of bed he ushered into my presence a squat bandy-legged individual with a round Mongolian face called On Khotaung who was apparently to look after me in the future. Pip did not seem to approve of On Khotaung very much, but I learned later he had a distinct bias against any orderly who was not a Gurkha. The Kukis in the Assam Rifles were generally magnificent people. Whereas the Gurkhas in a great many cases were only enlisted because they were either too young or too old to be accepted as recruits in an ordinary Gurkha Regiment, the Nagas and Kukis until the outbreak of war had no alternative unit in which to enlist and were generally of a very high quality.

I made tentative enquiries about washing and found Pip very noncommittal on the subject. Situated as we were on the summit of a high mountain it was necessary to descend a considerable distance before one came to water. It was thus difficult enough to keep the camp supplied with drinking water let alone provide the sahibs with baths. I ordered On Khotaung to go down to the stream and bring me back a tin of water with which to wash. He departed looking very sullen and was away for over an hour. When he finally returned there were great beads of perspiration on his forehead and he was showing signs of exhaustion which were probably somewhat exaggerated for my benefit. I did however sympathise with him and for ever afterwards while we were in that camp went unwashed like Pip.

The more I saw of Pip the more I realized what an intelligent and indomitable person he was. By nature and upbringing he was obviously a clean person, bur he had trained himself to keep working in conditions of indescribable filth. He had a theory that gymshoes were the ideal footwear for a V Force officer in that they would give him increased mobility across country, but as a result his feet were a hideous mass of jungle sores rather ineffectively covered with dirty little pieces of sticking plaster. He

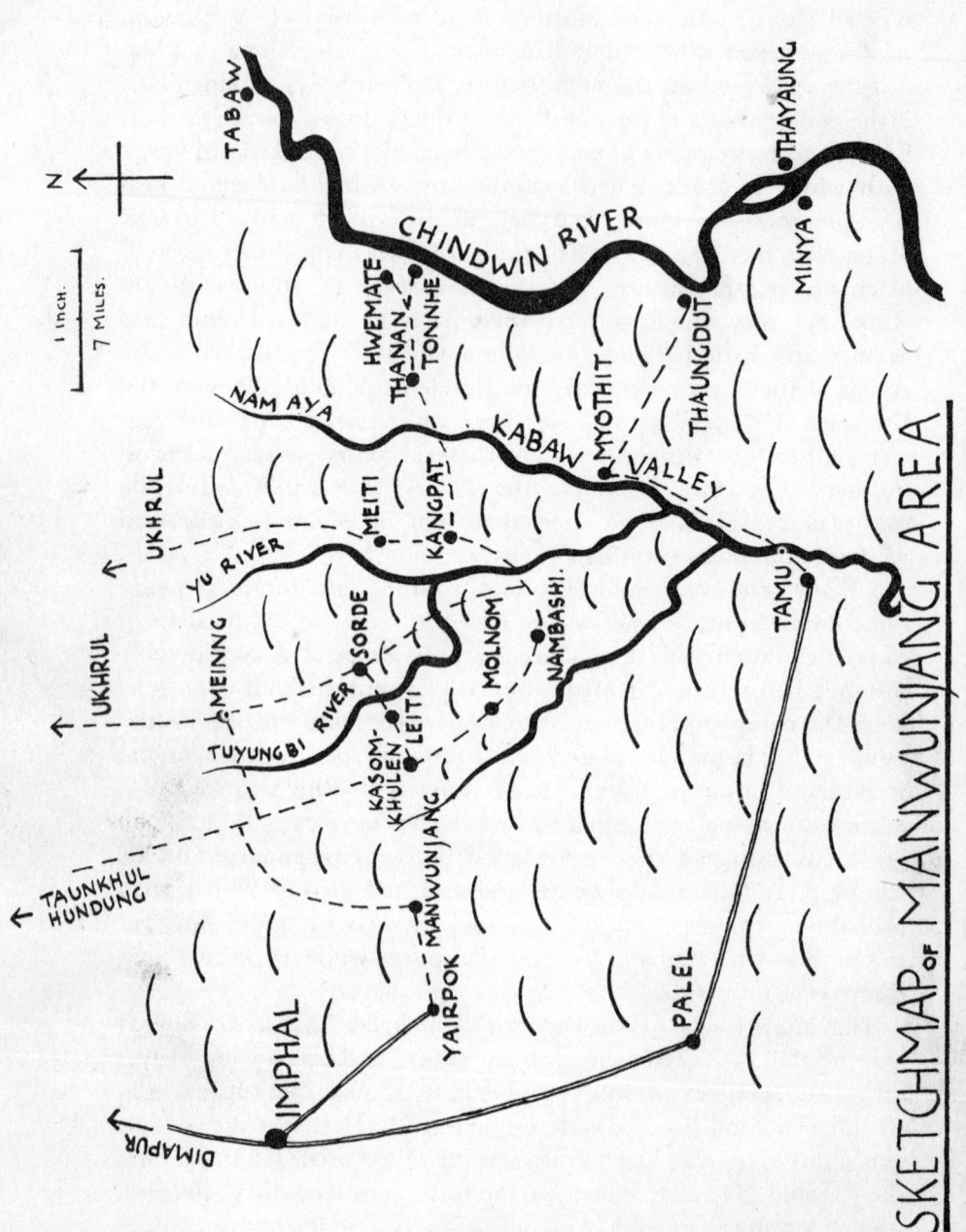

SKETCHMAP of MANWUNJANG AREA

1 INCH.
7 MILES.

N

DIMAPUR
IMPHAL
YAIRPOK
MANWUNJANG
PALEL

TAUNKHUL HUNDUNG

UKHRUL
UKHRUL

MEINNG
TUYUNGBI RIVER
KASOM-KHULEN
LEITI
SORDE
MOLNOM
NAMBASHI.

YU RIVER

MEITI
KANGPAT

NAM AYA

KABAW
VALLEY

MYOTHIT

TAMU.

THAUNGDUT

HWEMATE
THANAN
TONNHE

CHINDWIN RIVER

TABAW

THAYAUNG

MINYA

had apparently been suffering from recurrent bouts of malaria since his return from the Chindwin and was continually doping himself with quinine which is a much more drastic form of suppressive treatment than the ordinary mepacrin issued to the Army. Pip should have been on sick leave many weeks before and it was only his tremendous sense of duty that kept him going. During the retreat into Imphal most of the Officers in 3 V Ops had either been killed or become casualties through sickness and at that time Pip was alone on operations. He was due to go on leave as soon as I had learned sufficient of the business to run the sub-area on my own.

For the day's work we descended to the guard house below the camp and settled ourselves at a bamboo table in the bigger of the two huts. In the other hut a succession of Kukis and Nagas came and went and three Assam Riflemen prepared an endless succession of cups of tea. Pip arranged a set of maps that he had glued together against the wall of the hut and began to put me into the picture. He had been the Intelligence Officer of 3 V Ops for some time and explained himself well.

Mawunjang was situated on a less accessible route into the mountains and so far no Japs had penetrated very far into our area. To the east of us it was five days' march to the Kabaw Valley which runs parallel to the Chindwin Valley and was at that time teeming with Japs retreating from Ukhrul to the north and the Palel-Tamu track to the south. In both places the regular troops were in close contact with the enemy. Pip's role was largely intelligence. He was to provide timely information to 4 Corps in Imphal if the enemy started to move towards the plain through Manwunjang, and he was to organise a network of agents as far as possible into the Jap lines in the Kabaw Valley. In addition he intended in the next few days to take out a fighting force to strike at the enemy where he found them on our immediate front.

We discussed the tribal problems in the area. V Force had originally been raised along the Eastern Frontier of India as a post-occupation force which would remain behind in a guerilla role if the enemy advanced. For this purpose a number of shot guns had been issued to villagers in the early days and since the enemy crossing of the Chindwin Pip had obtained and issued

about forty rifles. The Civil Government had been very reluctant
to see the tribes armed, and had insisted on a very complete arms'
register being maintained of where and to whom we issued
weapons. To own or possess a firearm was the highest ambition of
every hillman and apart from any question of whether these arms
would be used against the enemy our power to issue them was a
most useful bait with which to induce Kukis and Nagas to make
journeys into the Jap lines in search of information.

During the morning some Nagas came in from Taunkhul
Hundung about a day's journey to the north to collect arms that
Pip had promised them. Some of them were tall and wore red
woollen blankets round their shoulders and had their heads shaved
at the sides and their hair swept back in a long mane across the
back of their heads. Others had short hair and wore a strange
mixture of coloured civilian shirts and khaki shorts. Pip explained
that the latter were Christian Nagas converted by the American
Baptist Mission that had worked in the hills before the war. In the
early days of V Force there had been a prejudice against the
Christian Nagas. Not being *zoo* drinkers it was alleged that they
lacked the stamina imparted by this beverage and that they were
of a more timid disposition and less suited to fighting than the
animists. But Pip's own views changed completely during the
invasion. On his long walk back from the Chindwin it was the
Christian Nagas who had helped him, hid him and fed him even
under the noses of the Japs, but the animists had always been too
petrified with fear to be of any real assistance.

Hitherto there had been no V Force organisation in the Naga
villages, but since Pip's return to the hills a few weeks before the
headmen had signified their willingness to fight. They were
alarmed at the way the more enterprising Kukis had been issued
with arms and at the stories of Jap foraging parties' activities in
the hill villages above the Kabaw valley. Pip had sent out messages
to them asking them to attend a meeting at a time and place to be
chosen by them at which he might settle a plan of campaign.

At ten o'clock we returned to the upper camp for the morning
meal which took the form of a curried bully beef and rice stew.
We ate with Pip's Anglo-Burmese wireless operator Webster. He
was a cheerful intelligent fellow whose father had been missing

since the Burma retreat. When we returned to the guard house there was an impassive looking Naga waiting for Pip with a message. Mani Ram translated it for us. It informed Pip that the Naga headmen were gathering at Kasom Khulen, a village about three hours' march down the track to the Kabaw Valley, and asked him to attend a meeting with them that evening.

2

In the Manipur hills the paths are much more intelligently arranged than in the Arakan. Wherever possible they follow the crests of the ranges instead of the beds of the streams in the valleys. The distances that one covers between the villages are often greater than need be, but the going is generally as level as can be contrived. From Manwunjang if one looks east on a fine day it is possible to see Kasom Khulen on the other side of a deep valley through which a mountain stream passes two thousand feet below. But the main track follows the line of the mountains north towards Taunkhul Hundung and then bears right across a col in a wide circle through the hills round the valley with the stream.

Pip and I set off at half past two with Mani Ram and four Gurkhas. Pip's long raking stride was as effective on level ground as it was on a hill and we were soon well ahead of the rest of the party. The Gurkhas are themselves slow methodical walkers and were a good excuse for me to beg for short halts at regular intervals. Towards the end of the journey it started to rain and a thick blanket of mist formed around us over the mountain. The last two miles were slightly downhill.

Kasom Khulen is a big village of about twenty houses and our visit was evidently something of an occasion. The *kalackwa* welcomed Pip clad in a bright scarlet blanket that had been presented to him by the Indian Government as a reward for long and meritorious service in his office. He carried a long ceremonial spear which he handed to a young spearman standing behind him when he came forward to greet us. We were taken to a large hut at the north end of the village where we were offered the inevitable *zoo*. I was very tired after the march and not yet acclimatised to the altitude and felt a delicious lassitude creeping through my whole body. Pip became involved in a series of interminable interviews with a party of Kuki scouts who came to see him without any apparent reason and I felt my head nodding from time to time.

'What did the Kukis want?' I asked him sleepily when he had at last got rid of them. He had been speaking Gurkhali and I had not understood.

'They want to find out just what's going on in Kasom Khulen.'

'What did you tell them?'

'I told them not too politely to go to hell'.

'I suppose the Kukis had to know about your meeting with the Nagas.'

'I suppose so. Probably most of the Kuki scouts in our camp at Manwunjang keep their friends well posted with what is going on. This is politics and much more interesting to them than the Jap war.'

'When's the meeting start?'

'Not until to-night. They'll probably kill a pig and we'll have a big meal and more *zoo* before the talking starts.'

I went to sleep for an hour and then Pip's orderly brought us tea. When I had drunk it I took my towel and a piece of soap out of my rucksack and made my way up hill to a stream I had seen just north of the village on our journey from Manwunjang. I felt that any opportunity for a wash when one was operating with Pip was not to be missed. The water had been collected from further up the side of the mountain and carried down to the track by a system of piping made out of hollowed bamboo. I stripped to my under pants and sat under the bamboo pipe and let the water run over my body. It was ice-cold and made my flesh tingle pleasantly. When I got back to the village I was feeling very wide awake and ready for anything. Even Pip was inspired to go off and follow my example.

For the evening's festivities the Nagas had killed a little grey mountain pig. These feed from the offal and refuse of the villages and are practically the only sanitary device known in the hills. After the Japs killed off the pigs in the villages one noticed at once how the places began to smell. But the pigs taste like any other kind of pork anywhere else in the world and as an alternative to the tinned diet on which we lived in the mountains they were a real delicacy. The pig had been roasted and not curried and was served with rice. With it we drank more rice beer and thus fortified set out for the meeting in a pleasantly mellow frame of mind. The *kalackwa* showed us the way by the light of a burning brand which he carried before us in his hand in very dramatic fashion.

The headmen had assembled in a large hut in the centre of the village. Pip and I seated ourselves in two very old and battered deck chairs that had been produced miraculously for the occasion in front of a roaring log fire. Mani Ram stood beside us ready to translate. Round the edges of the room the Nagas squatted like a set of graven images in a large circle. The light of the fire caught the bright colouring of their red and white blankets attractively.

In spite of his youth Pip handled the situation with great dignity. He chatted with me and smoked a cigarette while we drank two bottles of *zoo* that had been set before us and then rose to his feet just at the moment when I could sense from the atmosphere that everyone present was expecting him to start. He spoke in Gurkhali for the benefit of Mani Ram and the few ex-Assam Riflemen in the audience, pausing after every few sentences to allow Mani Ram to translate his words into Manipuri. Everything he said was very straightforward. He told the Nagas that he realized that they were faced with many difficult problems and that he was there to help them in any way he could. He told them that the tide of battle was now turning in favour of the British and that the Dimapur—Imphal road would soon be open again. Having thus opened the meeting, he sat down and left the headmen to continue the discussion.

There was no hesitation from any of the Naga speakers nor was there any unnecessary verbosity. One after another in an order that was either prearranged or based on some secret order of precedence in the hill country lean wrinkled hillmen came forward into the arc of light cast by the fire and made their speeches in a direct and very attractive manner. After they had finished Mani Ram translated the gist of what they had said to Pip and me. They were all very concerned at recent reports from the Kabaw Valley. The Japanese had been coming up into the villages in the mountains in search of food and laying the country completely waste. As the nearest villages to the enemy escape route from the Ukhrul area had been eaten bare, so they had advanced further and further into the hills. The headmen asked for regular troops to

be sent from Imphal to garrison the villages. They offered to feed
them out of their own rice stocks.

Pip explained that he had asked for a company of regular troops
to be sent into the mountains but that the generals had said that it
was quite impossible. The troops could not be everywhere in
Manipur at the same time and it was better to keep them
concentrated together in areas from which they could operate in
great strength. He offered as an alternative to arm the Nagas
themselves and said that the two of us would personally join their
levies with the twenty Assam Riflemen that we had with us in
Manwunjang. He said that this was the moment to oppose the Japs
and that if they could be made to realize that every village in the
mountains was against them and would resist them, they would
not dare to forage far from the Kabaw Valley itself. He promised
that in three days' time he would himself take what force he had
in Manwunjang against the Japanese.

The headman of Kasom Khulen, who seemed by mutual
consent to have been chosen as principal spokesman for everyone
present, rose to speak. He was calm, but what he said was
obviously very important to him. Mani Ram translated after he
had finished.

'He says the Nagas will fight the Japanese. They will choose
young men to enlist in the levies and carry arms. And if the British
send troops they will be fed by the villagers without any payment
being required. But they do not wish to serve in the same levies as
the Kukis. They cannot trust the Kukis and feel that they may be
betrayed to the Japs by them.'

Pip gazed for a while into the fire in meditation after the
headman's speech had been translated for him. Then he rose to his
feet and answered:

'Tell them,' he said to Mani Ram, 'that there shall be a separate
Naga levy which will never be called upon to serve side by side
with the Kukis. This will be organised during the next few days
under a leader that shall be chosen by the headmen themselves.
Together we will now fight the Japanese and drive him out of
Manipur.'

As Pip and I walked back to the hut where we were to sleep a
light rain was falling. Pip looked tired and very sad. He was

worrying about whether the Nagas would get any support or
thanks from the Indian Government for agreeing to fight the
Japanese. There was a good deal of jealousy and mistrust between
the civil authorities and V Force.

In the morning the headman of Nambashi came to see us before
we returned to Manwunjang. He was a little wizened old man with
an eighteen-year old son called Miba who had been one of the few
Nagas to join V Force in the early days. His village was about a
day's march down the track to the Kabaw Valley and in between
it and Kasom Khulen there was a Kuki village called Molnom. He
said that he had not approached us the previous night as he had
not wished to interrupt the meeting with a matter that concerned
his village alone, but that the headman of Molnom was stopping
the messengers that he sent from time to time to Manwunjang
with information about the enemy. The Kukis in Molnom had a
few firearms that had at one time been issued to them by V Force
and the Nagas had been threatened with these. Pip was white with
fury when he heard this news. When we reached Manwunjang at
midday he sent off a message to the headman of Molnom telling
him to come in to report.

But before the headman of Molnom had time to reach Manwunjang, we had set out for the Kabaw Valley. Fifteen fresh Assam
Riflemen arrived from Imphal the day we returned to our camp,
but Pip, who knew most of the battalion individually by that time,
decided that the ones already with us were the more likely men
for a raid, and accordingly the newcomers were with a few
exceptions left behind. The Assam Rifles had in peacetime been a
frontier police battalion, but since V Force had first been raised
they had been used to stiffen the levy cadres among the Nagas and
Kukis and in this capacity they had done some magnificent work.
All of them could speak enough Manipuri to be able to operate on
their own in the hills. This party was commanded by a tiny little
Gurkha Jemedar* called Gopal Thapa and under him there were
two Havildars.† One of these was an impressive looking thick-set

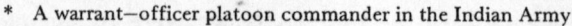

* A warrant—officer platoon commander in the Indian Army
† A sergeant in the Indian Army

Gurung who had won the IDSM during the retreat from the Chindwin and the other a rather elderly fellow with a slightly hunched back who I always referred to as 'The Spider King' because I could never remember his name. To make up the rest of the party Pip chose fourteen of the strongest Riflemen.

We spent a day cleaning and testing our weapons and deciding just what we would take with us. I threw away the battered old bush hat that I had had with me ever since my early days in the Arakan and adopted the Gurkha habit of wearing a cap comforter on my head. In addition to the big .45 American automatic with which all V Force officers were issued I borrowed a Sten gun and two magazines. It was decided that we would live on the country as far as possible, but we each carried two days' field scale rations in our packs as a reserve.

Pip's plan was to march down to Kasom Khulen along the main track and then take to the field paths that wound up and down over the mountains as the crow flies. The going on these field paths would be very hard, but on them we were much more likely to get into Japanese territory without being spotted. We left very early in the morning and marched down to Kasom Khulen. While we were eating in the village Pip sent out Naga scouts in all directions to find out the situation in front. He was very anxious to avoid passing through Molnom, as he felt that our presence would almost certainly be given away as a result. Due east of Kasom Khulen the ground fell steeply to another small Naga village called Leite and below that there was a mountain stream called the Tuyungbi River running south-east to join the Yu River in the Kabaw Valley. As it was very early in the monsoon the locals believed that we would be able to ford the stream and climb the hills on the other side of the valley to another Naga village called Sorde whence we should be in striking distance of the heights above the Kabaw Valley where the Japs were beginning to forage.

I spent most of that day lying on my back in a hut in Kasom Khulen listening to Pip and Mani Ram discussing the situation with the local Nagas. Then towards evening we moved down the hillside towards Leite guided by an eight-year old boy. Pip decided to sleep the night in the jungle. I told him that I thought we might be more comfortable in the village, but he insisted that we should be badly bitten by fleas. In the end we built ourselves a bivouac a little beyond the village and off the track. Pip and I arranged an elaborate shelter out of groundsheets and stretched out an old anti-gas cape beneath us. It was fairly chilly without blankets even though it had grown much warmer as we descended the hill, but I went off to sleep easily enough. At about two o'clock in the morning, however, a heavy shower of rain started to fall. Every one woke up and started cursing. I tried to pretend to myself that it was not really raining and then that it was not raining hard enough to matter and then a great pool of water formed beneath Pip and me and after that we gave up any attempt to sleep.

At dawn On Khotaung Kuki went up to the village to make tea and we all ate a packet of biscuits apiece. The villagers sent scouts to Sorde on the other side of the valley and we settled down to wait. We waited all that morning and I smoked innumerable pipes and became rather bored. I am not nearly such a methodical person as Pip and felt that he was really being far too systematic.

Then two Nagas arrived from Sorde in a state of high excitement with the news that there was a Jap foraging party moving in that direction. Pip decided that if we delayed our departure till the following morning we were almost bound to reach the village too late to do anything to forestall the Japs, so he ordered a night march. We set off downhill at about six o'clock and it grew dark about an hour later.

The first part of the journey was fairly easy going downhill but as we neared the bank of the river the atmosphere became very sticky and oppressive and rather like entering a hot house. We were moving across open ground where there had been a Naga *jume* farm and there was a full moon. But for about three or four hundred yards above the river there was a belt of thick jungle and once we entered this it was extremely dark. On the river bank there was a good deal of coughing and whispering and I realised that whatever virtues these little Assam Riflemen might have they were not as well-disciplined as regular infantry.

The river was running very fast but I never learned how deep it was for there was a stone causeway built across it from which the villagers fished until the monsoon swept it away each year and we scrambled across this without wetting our feet. On my arrival on the other side I discovered to my dismay that my automatic had dropped out of its holster during the journey downhill, but I still had my Sten gun with its two magazines.

The second half of the journey to Sorde was a nightmare that I shall remember all my life. I was starting to feel tired and the going deteriorated badly. The guides who were with us lost the track through the jungle in the darkness and we struggled violently up a precipitous hillside through fairly dense jungle for about two hours. Twice I thought that I was falling the full distance back into the *chaung* below but on each occasion I attached myself to a tree trunk at the last moment. Then we came out into the open Sorde *kheti* and the going improved. But the hillside was still very steep and every step I took I felt that I was going to collapse. The muscles in my calves were starting to bind. Even the Gurkhas seemed in the last stages of exhaustion. Finally Pip who was in front called a halt. I lumbered another hundred yards to the head of the column panting horribly and feeling very grotesque fell onto the ground beside him. In the moonlight I looked so comic that he burst out laughing.

'What happens now?' I whispered when I had regained my breath.

'We sleep till dawn.'

'Thank God!'

I crawled into a tiny *kheti* hut and stumbled over an elderly Naga asleep inside. About six Gurkhas had already established themselves in the place and two of them were already snoring. I lay down in a very cramped position partly overlaying my nextdoor neighbours, but no one seemed to mind and I was soon far away in a deep dreamless sleep. Pip woke me at dawn. I was feeling very stiff and was covered with dew.

'There are Japs in the village,' he said.

'How far away is that?'

'About a mile.'

'What's the next move?'

'We go on up the hill and contact the villagers. They'll know the best routes in.'

I shook myself out of my early morning torpor and found that my legs were moving more freely than a few hours before. We climbed a few hundred yards to the top of the *kheti* and shortly afterwards reached the watershed. There was a track running north along this which we followed. Half a mile further on we came to the ceremonial wooden gateway that one finds at the entrance of all Naga villages. It is a survival from the days when each village was surrounded by a stockade. All the men of the village were assembled there carrying spears and bottles of *zoo*. After my night in the open I felt that this was just what I needed and drank greedily.

As far as Pip could make out there were two parts to Sorde village, one inhabited by the Christians and called Khunou and one by the animists and called Kunbe. The latter was nearest to us and there were seven Japs cooking rice in one of the houses. They had apparently posted a sentry on the main track but the Nagas said they could guide us past him through the jungle. Pip divided up the party. The Jemedar Gopal and two Bren gun teams were to move off with a guide and to take up a position between the Christian and animist villages. Pip and I with five Assam Riflemen apiece were to move round to the left bypassing the sentry with more guides and then to rush the village. As I had the longest route to cover Pip arranged that he would not advance into the village until he heard my party begin to shoot. He gave me the Havildar with the IDSM to accompany me and took Mani Ram and the Spider King himself.

As I approached the village the Naga boy who was acting as our guide waved his hand nervously in the direction of the houses and disappeared the way he had come. On that first raid I felt cooler than I ever felt on similar occasions afterwards, probably because I was not in command of the operation. It all seemed very simple. I had been told to move quietly into the village and start shooting and that is what I did. As I came out of the jungle and into the houses I saw a man in a pair of khaki shorts walking across my front with a waterbottle in his hand. He did not see us. I tapped the Assam Rifleman on my right on the arm and signalled to him to shoot. He aimed, fired and missed. The Jap halted in his tracks and stood as if frozen. Just as I was beginning to wonder whether he had been hit after all and would fall to the ground at any moment I saw his head turn. I opened up with my Sten gun but it jammed after firing two rounds. He turned towards us and saw me and for a second I was glad that I had missed him for there was death in his eyes. He darted through the stilts on which a nearby hut stood and out into the jungle beyond and down the hillside. There his luck failed him for he ran straight into Pip's party advancing up the slope and was hit as he ran.

Furious with myself and the Gurkha, I advanced into the village. The Havildar with the IDSM was nowhere to be seen but two Assam Riflemen were still beside me. As we came to each house I poured a burst through the wooden walls while the two Gurkhas covered the exits, but all the Japs had gone. In one hut we found two very rusty British Sten guns and some odds and ends of Japanese equipment with a pilot's map of the area.

At this stage Pip appeared on the scene. He had heard the shooting and thought it better not to advance into the village while it was going on. The Havildar with the IDSM and the two other Assam Riflemen with him had completely disappeared. For a few minutes we gave way to the temptation which assails all troops after they have reached an objective and sat down and smoked a cigarette hoping that everyone else would appear at any moment. This nearly led to disaster.

Suddenly there was a loud report from the edge of the jungle about ten yards behind Pip and he collapsed hurriedly into some nearby undergrowth. Mani Ram fired a burst with his Sten gun in the direction from which the shot had come. One of the Japs that we had chased out of the village had evidently come back up the hill through the undergrowth to see what was going on and taken the opportunity to take a shot at Pip. Fortunately he had missed, but it was obviously unhealthy to remain in the village, so we set off in the direction of the Christian village to collect Jemedar Gopal and his Bren gun teams.

As we moved we heard several bursts of automatic fire from that direction and we had hardly gone more than a hundred yards before the Jemedar's party arrived with the news that the Christian village was alive with Japanese. Shortly after my party had started shooting a party of about twenty of these had come down the track to investigate and run straight into the Jemedar's ambush. He had not stayed to count the bodies, but he was quite convinced that his two Bren guns had hit the party fairly hard. We were all very anxious to contact the missing Havildar and his two Riflemen, but it was obviously extremely dangerous to remain where we were, so we withdrew into the jungle on the hillside for about four hundred yards and lay up for the rest of the day. Pip sent two patrols to search the hillside west of the village for the missing men but there was no trace of them.

Some of the local Nagas, who were all living with their families in some *kheti* huts about a mile from the village, brought us rice. They said that the seven Japs whom we had attacked in the village had been an advance party that had moved in by moonlight to prepare a meal for a larger party that was following behind them. These had numbered about a hundred and fifty and had actually arrived in the Christian village just after the attack began. We held a conference of war. The Japs had already discovered the Nagas' rice stores and were gorging themselves to their satisfaction. They were now in a very suspicious mood and there were apparently sentries everywhere. Pip was a little depressed about what had happened. We had lost three men. The Japs had plundered the rice stores. And there seemed little chance of our taking them by surprise for that day at any rate. On the credit side we had killed a few Japs and caused them a certain amount of irritation.

After dark Pip decided that there was no point in remaining in the area any longer and we set off down the hill and across the *kheti*. We were all very tired and I was angry with myself for missing such an easy shot earlier in the day and about the coughing and unnecessary noise that the men were making. On the far side of the *kheti* we moved a little way into the jungle and settled down for the night. Pip remembered how difficult it had been climbing up through the jungle above the river even in moonlight and did not wish to make the return journey until next day. We were all dog tired and very hungry and to cap our misfortunes it began to rain. At dawn we moved on down to the river bank and crossed the causeway of stones. The river had risen in the night. Much to my delight one of the Gurkhas found my big Colt automatic lying on the ground on the other side.

The climb up to Leite was very hard work. We had lost all the nervous energy that had helped us forward to Sorde in the night march, and a deep depression had settled upon us. But in the village we found the missing Havildar and the two men. He had been hit by a bullet in the arm. Just after I had advanced into the village a party of Japs had appeared on our left flank and he had had a gun battle with them while I was moving about among the houses. After he had been hit he had withdrawn down the slope towards the river with his two men. Fortunately his wound was not a bad one and we were able to evacuate him to Imphal on his own feet.

Back in the camp at Manwunjang we found four very thin and emaciated Sikhs. They were deserters from the Japanese sponsored Indian National Army Division that had gone into action along the Tamu-Palel track. All of them had originally been prisoners of war in Malaya. But by a combination of threats and starvation rations they had been induced to turn traitor. They can never have been very effective troops on the side of the Japanese, for they had escaped on the first opportunity that had occurred. They were obviously very impressed by the rations that the Gurkhas were eating. They told us that in the Kabaw Valley they and their Japanese masters were reduced to starvation fare.

Next day Pip walked down the mountain to attend a conference at Corps Headquarters, having previously arranged by wireless that a truck from Imphal should meet him in Yairipok. He took the INA Sikhs with him. While he was away a series of very alarming reports began to come in from the Naga villages on the opposite side of the Tuyungbi River. After our departure from Sorde the Japs had occupied the village in force and taken hostages from among the inhabitants until such time as Tipa, an eighteen-year old Naga schoolmaster, who was the local V Force leader and had guided us into the village, should surrender himself to them.

The enemy had spread eastwards into the little triangle of hills between the Tuyungbi and Yu Rivers and were plundering and burning and killing wherever they went. Every day pathetic little columns of Naga and Kuki refugees arrived in Kasom Khulen. It was the custom among the hillmen that each village should feed travellers sheltering within its walls overnight. This was an excellent and civilised arrangement under normal circumstances, but was becoming impossible at that time.

I wirelessed Pip in Imphal explaining how bad matters were becoming. Fortunately for the whole countryside the monsoon had broken in all its fury after the Sorde raid and the river had become overnight a swirling torrent that it was quite impossible to cross. All our intelligence sources beyond it had gone dead. When I first joined Pip he was daily receiving information as to what was going on as far away as in the Kabaw Valley itself, but now the Nagas had evacuated the whole area east of the Tuyungbi River.

A great blanket of mist had descended onto the mountain around us and day after day the rain fell almost continuously. The track down to the guard post had been badly broken up and was deep in mud. Everywhere the local population seemed on the verge of starvation. Pip wirelessed from Imphal that the civil government had arranged a rice distribution point at the foot of the mountains in Yairipok, but this was in Manipuri country and I found that the hillmen seemed frightened to go there. What they feared most was that they might be obliged to abandon their independent way of life in the mountains, rigorous though it might be, and to work as coolies in the Imphal plain.

I was very glad when Pip returned. He had enjoyed his well deserved break and was looking much fitter than when I had first met him. He brought news that the road to Dimapur had been opened and that a stream of lorries was pouring into Imphal with ammunition, petrol, rations and other supplies. He also brought rum, tobacco and cigarettes and that night there were some very contented faces in the camp. In the afternoon we received information that a party of six Indians had arrived in Kasom Khulen. A Lance-Naik* and two Assam Riflemen were sent down to investigate and towards nightfall they returned with the strangers, who turned out to be Punjabi Musalmen from the INA led by a lieutenant who had been a Jemedar in the British service in Malaya. He was by far the most intelligent observer that we had so far interrogated as to what was actually going on in the Kabaw Valley. He had belonged to a Sapper and Miner Company that had been building a road from Tamu to Sittaung. After the monsoon had started this had developed into a quagmire and although they had been driven mercilessly by the Japs a large number of motors had become hopelessly immobilised. The Jemedar confirmed the reports that the Japs were in pitiful condition. By that time they all realised that their attempt to capture Imphal had failed and many of them had not had a square meal in weeks. There were no

*A Lance-Corporal in the Indian Army.

medical services and the paths were littered with the bodies of men who had been left to die.

While I was with V Force more than a dozen escaped INA men passed through my hands. I found that they fell into two categories. Firstly, there was an element who were ex-prisoners of war from Malaya. These were more politically minded than the average Punjabi Sepoy and for the most part innocuous, but completely degraded by their experiences. Secondly, there was a small element recruited from the Indian civilian population domiciled in Malaya and Burma before the war. These often spoke a little English and were much more dangerous material.

If one accepted the surrender of an INA soldier one was required to fill in a form in which he was graded as White, Grey or Black, according to the extent to which he had been tainted by enemy influences. I never graded a man as Black, even though he was a domiciled-Indian civilian from Malaya or Burma, as I considered that this treatment should be reserved for men who were captured in actual combat against us. But I was at the same time loth to brand any of them as White, as they had all served as soldiers of the Jap forces and must to some extent have come under their influence. I therefore adopted the practice of grading every one of them as Grey, until one day after I became a parachutist my party was joined by an escaped Gurkha who had been on the run in the Karen hills from the time of the original Burma retreat. He actually fought beside my men against the enemy, and although he had admitted having served in the Japanese sponsored police force in Burma I sent him in to Army Headquarters as a White.

On the strength of the Jemedar's report and the re-opening of the Imphal—Dimapur road Pip decided to start moving his headquarters forward to Kasom Khulen. He and I moved the following day, and the wireless and rear party were to follow later. There had been a small V Force camp in the early days on the eastern edge of the village and this had been repaired in readiness for us by the *kalackwa*. The evening we arrived the headman of Molnom appeared looking very much ashamed of himself and carrying a peace offering of a chicken done up in a little bamboo cage. He apologised for not coming before but told us that one of his villagers, a man called Chunkohem, who had been at one time a scout in V Force but had gone over to the Japs after the invasion of Manipur, had until recently been living in the village and would have brought reprisals on the villagers if they had not appeared to favour the Japanese. The very fact that the headman should have come in to report suggested that he knew that the Japanese were already defeated. Pip finally forgave the old man and sent him back to his village. But the Naga refugees all wanted to kill him.

Hardly had the headman of Molnom departed than our old friend the *kalackwa* of Nambashi appeared. He also brought a present of a chicken trussed up in a little bamboo cage together with a bottle of *zoo*, and we realised at once that something was amiss. After the customary greetings, he informed Pip through Mani Ram that there was a large party of marauding Japs about five miles east of his village. Pip assured the old man that the Japanese had been heavily defeated at Imphal and were all withdrawing hot foot for the Chindwin River, but he remained unconvinced and kept begging for some *sipahi singh*, as he called the regular troops, to be sent to protect his village. There were at the time about fifty armed Nagas in Kasom Khulen, and Pip offered to send them down to Nambashi, but the *kalackwa* insisted that they would be quite useless if the Japanese came and in the end Pip offered to send a Lance-Naik and two Assam Riflemen with the party. This seemed to soothe the old man's nerves a little and he was looking quite cheerful again when he set out on his return journey to his village about an hour later with the ambush party, which was commanded by a Darjeeling Gurkha.

In fact both Pip and I were somewhat puzzled by the news brought from Nambashi. The headman had the reputation of being a stout-hearted old fellow and Pip felt that he would not have come to us for help without some good reason. North of his village there was a steel suspension bridge that crossed the Tuyungbi River, the only one in the area. We finally decided that the enemy concentration in the fork of the Tuyungbi and Yu Rivers might now be moving south instead of due east. An explanation for this might be that the Yu River was too swollen by monsoon water for them to be able to get across it.

We signalled some likely targets for air strikes to Assam Zone, and the following day we heard aircraft overhead, but the mist on the mountains was very thick and after they had circled for a little we heard them return in the direction of Imphal. It rained hard and we spent our time in the hut smoking and trying to work out crossword puzzles. After dark Pip forbade all lights in the camp, and we ate our meal in darkness and went to bed. About ten o'clock I could hear whispered consultations going on outside our hut and finally the Spider King came groping through the doorway.

'The ambush party has returned from Nambashi,' he told Pip.

'What d'you mean?' Pip snorted as he collected his senses. 'I told them to wait four days in the village.'

'The village is full of Japs.'

'Did the ambush party fight with them?'

'No, sahib, there were many Japs.'

Pip was furious. The unfortunate Lance-Naik was shown into his presence and the rather disgraceful story unfolded. As in most Naga villages there was a Nambashi Kunbe and a Nambashi Khunou. The ambush party had been lying up in the former after its arrival and the latter had been occupied by the enemy about dusk. The first party of enemy to arrive had apparently numbered seventeen, a number that could well have been frightened away in the first instance by the Lance-Naik and his men. But they had withdrawn without firing a shot. All the villagers had come with them and a large supply of rice had been left to fall into enemy hands. Pip was obviously very concerned at the episode. After the camp had once more settled down for the night, we again heard someone in the doorway.

'Who's that?' asked Pip in a whisper.

'Lance-Naik Bom Bahadur Chettri.'

This was a jovial fellow with a great deal of gold in his teeth who was continually grinning. Chettris are not very popular in the Gurkha Brigade, because they of all the Gurkha castes are nearest to the Indians. But this man was an excellent soldier.

'What d'you want?' asked Pip.

'I want to take a fighting patrol down to Nambashi, sahib.'

'Why?'

'Listen, sahib, that fellow who came back is a Darjeeling

Gurkha. In Darjeeling they're a yellow livered set of bastards. I'm from across the border in Nepal. Let me take some men down tomorrow and we'll knock hell out of those Japs. For the honour of the regiment, please let me go.'

This was just the sort of approach to the situation that was best calculated to appeal to Pip with his public school code of honour. I could tell when he next spoke that he was very pleased that Bom Bahadur should have made the request he had.

'You can take two Assam Riflemen and as many Nagas as you like with you and leave at dawn,' he said.

Early next morning the inhabitants of Nambashi began to arrive in Kasom Khulen. Each of them carried a large bamboo basket containing what few personal belongings they had been able to salvage. It looked a pathetic enough little procession. Both Pip and I felt very angry and also extremely helpless. We drafted the daily situation report and another message on the subject of the rice shortage that was developing in the area and sent them off to Webster and the wireless set at Manwunjang by runner.

Then Lance-Naik Bom Bahadur Chettri came bouncing into the office hut with a broad grin on his face and gave an extravagant parade ground salute. He asked for permission to march in his best Gurkha manner. The etiquette of soldiering is very dear to Gurkhas and they never neglect it, even in the most improbable situations. He had chosen as his companions a Kuki called Lenji in the Assam Rifles and another Gurkha from Nepal with a Bren gun, and in addition twenty-five Naga boys armed with a motley collection of shotguns, and Lee Enfield rifles. Pip and I wished him luck, and told him not to take any unnecessary risks, and then he set off down the track in the direction of Molnom with his strange force straggling behind him in a long crocodile.

After he had gone Pip and I ate our breakfast of the inevitable curried bully beef and rice and settled down to wait. All day we read and talked and did crossword puzzles and listened to a new sound that we heard for the first time in those hills that day, the distant booming of artillery fire to the south. In the evening a runner came in from Webster with a packet of decoded messages that had been received over the wireless. One of them contained instructions for Pip to return to Imphal and proceed on leave. That night we had a farewell dinner off a tough little mountain chicken by way of a special treat and he left the following day shortly after dawn. Pip was an excellent companion and a good officer to work for and I was sorry to say good-bye to him.

The day was uneventful until about four o'clock in the afternoon when a tall and very ugly Kuki appeared in the doorway of my hut clad in the usual rather ragged white shirt. I looked up from the book I was reading wondering who on earth this unannounced stranger might be and was bewildered to see him bring up his right hand in a very smart orthodox military salute at the same time taking a short step backwards and closing his bare heels together in a silent imitation of the Guardsman's ceremonial. He greeted me in Gurkhali.

'Who are you?' I asked.

'Dumkou, sahib. Late of V Force. Once a Lance-Naik in the band of the Fourth Battalion of the Assam Rifles.'

'Where have you come from?'

'I have been a prisoner of the Japanese.'

Dumkou Kuki had been out in civilian clothes on an intelligence mission in the Kabaw Valley when he had run into a Japanese patrol that was being guided by a traitor Kuki called Chunkohem, who came from Molnom. Dumkou also owned land in Molnom and Chunkohem had known that he was working for V Force, but probably afraid lest he start a village feud, he had told the Japanese nothing about it. They had conscripted Dumkou as a coolie to carry rice for them and had finally set him to work as a cook in a staging camp in the village of Meiti on the other side of the Yu River. He had remained there for about three weeks and then made his escape one night when the Japanese had come to take his presence for granted.

By that time I was very suspicious of nearly all Kukis, unless they were enlisted in the Assam Rifles, but I decided to make an exception in the case of Dumkou, and told him that he might remain in the camp and do liaison work between myself and the Kukis. My orderly, On Khotaung, who knew him, seemed very pleased at this arrangement. He kept telling me whenever he was alone with me in the hut that there were many good and valuable men among the Kuki villagers and that those who were helping the enemy were very much exceptions to the rule that the Kuki peoples were loyal to the Government.

Dumkou told me that Molnom village was now empty and that all the villagers had taken refuge in the field huts. There were apparently several hundred Japanese three miles further down the track gorging themselves in the rice barns at Nambashi.

Towards nightfall a messenger arrived from Bom Bahadur's party. They had lain up around Molnom all day, but had seen nothing. They were going to withdraw to a small Naga village off the main track to shelter for the night. I sent him back a note written in Roman Urdu telling him to withdraw if there was any danger of his being encircled, as our primary task was intelligence and not slaughter and I did not want there to be any casualties. Then I ate my evening meal and settled down in the darkened hut to try to sleep. After a while On Khotaung appeared rather hesitantly in the doorway.

'Sahib.'

'Yes. What d'you want?'

'I want to go down to Molnom.'

'Why?'

'My wife lives in Molnom.'

'Why didn't you tell me this before?'

'I was afraid. Everyone was saying that the Molnom people are very bad.'

'Are they?'

'No, sahib.'

I sent for Dumkou and the Spider King, who was the senior NCO in the camp, and we had a lengthy discussion on what was to be done about On Khotaung's wife. The Spider King evidently did not approve of the Kuki element in the Assam Rifles, and saw no reason why anything should be done at all. Dunkou thought that she would be all right provided she was with the villagers, as they would all go into hiding in some remote part of the jungle if their village was occupied by the Japs. He agreed to go down to the village in Kuki dress the following night to find out what was going on, and if necessary bring her back with him. After this whispered discussion we all adjourned to bed.

In the morning another INA deserter arrived at Kasom Khulen. He was a big sullen Punjabi Musalman who apparently came from the same company of Sappers and Miners as the Jemedar. He laboured under a grievance against the Jemedar and kept on trying to explain to me just what a treacherous scoundrel the Jemedar was. I sent him back to the camp at Manwunjang with an Assam Rifleman and two Nagas in order to be rid of him.

When the daily runners arrived with the messages that Webster had received over the wireless the previous day, I learned that the Gurkha Parachute Battalion that had been working on the right flank of 20th Division at Ukhrul had moved south, and that there were Gurkhas in Taunkhul Hundung, a Naga village a long day's march to the north of us.

Afraid lest, if they came south, they might mistake my rather unorthodox force for enemy levies, I sent off two Nagas with a message to their commanding officer. I told him marauding Japs on my front had started to advance in my direction and that I might have to withdraw into his box. Corps were getting interested in my area. An enemy prisoner taken recently had stated on interrogation that the unit to which he belonged had received orders to take Yairipok. It was considered possible that as a last suicide venture the Japanese might try a rush through my area to the Imphal plain.

Then in the late afternoon a young Naga arrived at a run from Bom Bahadur's party. He was very excited and practically incoherent, but he spoke of a great battle having been fought between Bom Bahadur and the Japanese. About an hour later the Nagas began to arrive in twos and threes. Their faces were flushed with triumph and they had evidently had a success. At the tail came Lance-Naik Bom Bahadur and Lenji Kuki, who was carrying the Bren gun. They were both grinning broadly and very pleased with themselves. I led them into my hut out of a thin drizzle of rain that had set in, and pieced their story together.

That morning the ambush party had moved forward to Molnom and taken up a position at the crest of a steep hill east of the village. There they had waited in great misery throughout the day while heavy monsoon rain fell around them. At about three o'clock an enemy platoon had marched up the track in close formation. Bom Bahadur had sited his Bren gun close to the path with the Nagas stretched out on either side of him on the hillside in a crescent formation. He had waited until the Japs were about fifty yards away and then opened up. The enemy had been caught at a point on the path from which they could not easily escape into the jungle and the leading elements had taken heavy punishment. On either flank a great volume of inaccurate fire had come from the Nagas and the enemy had been seen to scatter in some confusion down the hill.

After this there had been a pause for half an hour while the enemy reorganised. Then they had opened fire on Molnom with a mortar and advanced in great strength. Bom Bahadur and his men had withdrawn fast. I congratulated him on what had obviously been a very effective little ambush, for which he was later awarded the Military Medal. When questioned as to the condition of the leading Japs, he was quite certain that they were wearing full equipment and in good condition. Some of the Naga scouts reported that there had been mules with the party.

That night I withdrew my headquarters from Kasom Khulen to Manwunjang, leaving only an ambush party of six Assam Riflemen supported by about fifty levies in the village with orders to withdraw themselves if the place was attacked. It was not a popular decision with the Nagas who were elated by the battle of the afternoon and convinced that if we remained the Japs would not dare to approach the village, but I felt that it was the only possible one in the circumstances. My little force was not designed for heavy defensive action against the enemy, and it was pointless to fight except upon ground and at a time of one's own choosing. But I have nevertheless sometimes felt that I should have stayed just because the Nagas wanted me to stay and they were such delightful, simple people. Fortunately, as it transpired, the Japs never came any further west than Molnom.

I soon realised that my decision to move at night was a great mistake. Except at the time of the full moon it is all but impossible to move along a path in those mountains after dark. Even such well-trained night fighters as the Japanese had advanced into the hills by the light of torches when they had first crossed the Chindwin. On that particular occasion not only was there no moon, but it was also raining very hard. The path along which we scrambled and slid was in the daytime as good a one as you find in that country, but we found it quite impossible. The tail of the column soon lost contact with those in front and after several of the other men and I had all slipped over the side of the hill and dropped a distance of about twenty feet into a tangled growth of bushes, I called a halt and we settled down as best we could in the jungle for the night. Next morning when we arrived in Man-wunjang we were all looking very tired and bad-tempered and I felt that I had made a fool of myself.

Webster sent through a situation report to Imphal, and I expanded it with a warning that if the Japs in Molnom were something more than a foraging party and were in fact advancing to capture Yairipok, they were in a position to reach their objective within forty-eight hours. I marked the message Top Priority. Then I went off to sleep in the hope that by the time I should awake the situation would have clarified itself. I slept for three hours.

Then the Spider King brought in a Naga with a message from the ambush party at Kasom Khulen. It was written in very badly phrased Roman Gurkhali and was to the effect that the Japs were still in Molnom, and that a platoon of Gurkhas had arrived in Kasom Khulen.

This last item was very puzzling as I had no information that there were any other Gurkhas in the area, and the idea occurred to me that perhaps an INA infiltration was taking place. But on further consideration I rejected this possibility as there were reputed to be very few Gurkhas in the INA. In the end I decided to go back to Kasom Khulen to find out for myself. I took the Spider King and six Assam Riflemen and left at three o'clock in the afternoon.

There were no women or children in Kasom Khulen as I walked up the main street and on to the V Force camp. In Naga country that is a sure sign of imminent trouble. In the camp there was a section of armed Naga levies and the rest of the party and the Assam Riflemen were out on the track to the east. I asked about the Gurkhas, using On Khotaung as my interpreter, and was told that they were living in a hut in the village. We all walked over to see them.

When I arrived they were busy boiling tea. Their commander was a Rai Havildar with a cheerful round Mongolian face.

'Who are you?' I asked.

'152 Parachute Battalion, sahib.'

'What orders did your officer give you?'

'He told us to come down here for five days.'

'There are several hundred Japs in the next village. What will you do if they come?'

'We shall stay here.'

'Did your officer tell you to do that?'

'Yes.'

Somewhat puzzled at these instructions, which I learned later were incorrectly repeated by the Havildar, I went back to the V Force camp and smoked a pipe while I considered the situation. The Spider King had had a touching reunion with a friend from his own village among the paratroops and had stayed to drink some tea. I decided that as long as the paratroops stayed in Kasom Khulen I myself would have to stay. In any case now that we were reinforced, the situation had improved considerably.

Next morning the Rai Havildar arrived outside my hut and asked permission to send out a fighting patrol.

'Where d'you want to send it?' I asked.

'Across the Tuyungbi River.'

'How are you going to get across?'

'The Nagas have built a bridge so that the families on the east bank can escape from the Japs.'

'How many men are you going to send?'

'Three.'

This small number rather surprised me, but I did not interfere and much to my surprise they brought in a prisoner that evening. He was a very tall thin Jap with a fair complexion and a sinister ingratiating smile. He had put up a tremendous struggle before he was disarmed and thrown three grenades all of which had failed to explode. But by the time he reached Kasom Khulen he was completely resigned to captivity. He spoke no language that any one present understood, and I was unable to get any information.

During the next two days we kept ambushes out in front along the Molnom track, but there were no signs of the enemy. They had captured a large store of rice and were too busy feeding themselves to think of a move. The RAF attempted an air strike, but were unable to find the target in the mist. Then 3 V Ops signalled that Corps were sending two brigades into the Manwunjang area. And the next day the Gurkha paratroop platoon was withdrawn north to Taunkhul Hundung. They were a magnificent body of troops and I was sorry to see them depart.

I moved all my men forward to Kasom Khulen except for Webster and a small rear party who remained in the old camp at Manwunjang with the wireless. West of our position on the heights above Yairipok the two brigades started to dig themselves in. Everyday it rained continuously and the trenches filled with water as soon as they had been dug. Owing to the streams on the lower slopes of the mountains being in spate it proved impossible to supply the regular troops by mule from the Imphal plain, and the mist made it extremely difficult for aircraft to drop supplies. The presence of the regular troops in such numbers disrupted my own supply arrangements and the parties of coolies which I sent down the hill to collect rations and stores were invariably commandeered by the military on the way for their own purposes. As a result I was very soon extremely short of rations.

Finally Corps decided to withdraw the two brigades from the mountains and retain a single Punjabi battalion with two companies of Gurkhas under command to push on down the main track through Molnom and Nambashi to the Kabaw Valley. I moved beside them and tried to make myself as useful as possible, but it was not an occasion on which a guerilla unit had any useful role. What fighting there was to be done was of the straight frontal variety that is best performed by regular troops, and there was little chance of achieving tactical surprise. I was, however, in a position to organise parties of Naga coolies as porters, and act as a liaison officer between the hill peoples and the regular troops. Moreover, the notorious Chunkohem, a Kuki who had collaborated with the Japs, came in and surrendered at this time. I told him that I was not in a position to secure a pardon for him, but that if he worked for me as well I would at any rate inform whoever should deal with his case eventually of his services, and that possibly these might go to mitigate any punishment that was coming to him. Twice I sent him into the Japanese occupied area as a spy. On both occasions he brought me back valuable information which was of assistance to the regular troops.

The Punjabis were commanded by an Indian Regular major, an excellent officer, whose old battalion had had to surrender in Singapore and who was very anxious to try and salvage as many of the INA as possible before they were withdrawn to the other side of the Chindwin. His battalion was held up in front of Molnom for about a week, and then just when a frontal attack was about to be launched the enemy withdrew.

At that stage the party of Assam Rifles that I had with me was replaced by a fresh platoon from Imphal and with these I crossed the Tuyungbi River by a suspension bridge built out of creepers that the Nagas were able to throw across the river in a break in the rains. With some Naga scouts moving in front we scrambled up a very precipitous path and attempted to surround a party of Japanese stragglers in the village of Meiring. Unfortunately we had failed to cover all the exits and all of them were able to escape into the jungle. On that occasion I realised once and for all how extraordinarily difficult it is to surround a jungle village successfully and how many men are required. The thought was afterwards very comforting to me when I found myself more concerned with whether I myself was likely to be surrounded.

About this time the Kuki villages decided that the British were really going to win the war and at last started to operate against the Japanese in earnest. There was nothing very heroic in the decision, as by then the enemy rearguards seemed to be in the last stages of exhaustion. It all began when two Kuki villagers from the country east of the Tuyungbi River brought in a Japanese rifle and some other equipment and reported to me that they had ambushed a party of enemy stragglers. I was pleased by the incident and gave them a reward in new silver rupee pieces to encourage further offensive activities. Three days later two separate parties of Kukis came in to see me with similar reports.

Although I paid out the rewards the suspicion arose at the back of my mind that here there was the makings of a very easy little racket. I had no real check on whether or not what they told me was true, and although the hill peoples were quite strikingly honest by comparison to the inhabitants of any other country that I had ever been in, I felt that it was subjecting them to undue temptation not to insist on some form of evidence of their deeds. So I passed out an instruction through the V Force scouts that in future I would only pay rewards in respect of Japs killed where the ears of the victim were laid before me as proof of the deed.

This proposal must have appealed to the Kukis. Within a week nearly a dozen pairs of Japanese ears had been brought into my hut at Kasom Khulen. I had with me at the time a very pleasant young Indian doctor called Mascarenhas who had come out from Imphal to see whether he could be of any assistance in the area. A devout Roman catholic and a man of kindly, gentle habits, he was appalled by what he saw. He felt, probably with justification, that the practice was calculated to lead one day to repercussions against our own troops.

The climax came one afternoon when I was out and a wicked looking little Kuki appeared in the camp carrying with him not only the ears but the nose and upper lip of a Japanese soldier wrapped up in a filthy little piece of cloth. In my absence he displayed his trophy to the scandalised doctor, pointing out the interesting fact that there were actually hairs on the upper lip. Mascarenhas refused the fellow his reward, and thereafter no further claims of that sort were made to us. I was in fact rather relieved.

After the Meiring raid a two-battalion column commanded by a full colonel passed through the Punjabis with orders to advance to the Chindwin River. This was held up for several days by floods in the Yu River. Some Kuki scouts of mine had been able to bridge the stream a few days earlier and I had sent a two-man reconnaissance patrol of Assam Riflemen across. But very heavy rain fell the following night and the bridge was carried away behind them in the spate of the stream. Fortunately the Japs had already evacuated the villages of Kangpat and Meiti on the heights above the Kabaw Valley. Finally some Sappers and Miners with the regular troops succeeded in passing a rope bridge across the river and my party with an infantry company were slung across.

In Kangpat I found the two Assam Riflemen who were practically starving. The village had been plundered bare by the Japs and not a grain of rice nor an animal remained. The inhabitants were living on roots which they collected in the jungle. That night the rope bridge broke behind us and we were held up until such time as the RAF could drop another. I sent down Kuki and Naga scouts to reconnoitre Thanan. A few days before we crossed the Yu River Chunkohem had made a journey down into the Kabaw Valley and confirmed that the final Jap line of withdrawal was across the Thanan—Tonnhe track, a route which Wingate had followed on the first Chindit operation, and as a result there was a big air strike on Thanan which was unfortunately a day late.

In Kangpat I was visited by the headman of the Kuki village of Meiti, a wicked looking old man who was reputed to have handed over an educated Naga girl who had been trained as a nurse in the American Baptist Mission to a Japanese officer as his mistress. Much to my surprise he informed me that when the invasion had started there had been a V Force rice store in his village, and that he had succeeded in hiding this throughout the period of the enemy occupation. It consisted of thirty-two bags of rice. As his villagers were near starvation, it seemed to be an act of great forbearance on his part. The rice was extremely welcome to me as I had had no rations issued to my party since leaving Kasom Khulen.

In the circumstances I made no move to arrest the headman of Meiti, but justice was not long delayed. There was in V Force a Naga officer called Kathing, the only member of his race to hold a commission in the Indian Army. In peacetime he had been the headmaster of the school in Ukhrul, and during the war he had become a legend in the Manipur hills. During the siege of Imphal he had compiled a list of collaborators among the hill tribes and while I was in Kangpat for a conference with the Naga and Kuki tribesmen a fortnight later some of Kathing's scouts came in and arrested the Meiti headman, leading him off to Imphal with his wrists bound.

On Khotaung, who had remained wih me at his own request when the remainder of his platoon returned to Imphal, suddenly announced that he had an uncle in Meiti and I gave him leave for one night to attend a *puja* in the village. When he returned he brought with him a bottle of rice spirit as a present for me. This is

not as strong as the ordinary Army issue rum, and it is a good
drink provided one does not savour it with one's nose beforehand,
for it gives off a very sickly odour. At the time I was unaware of
its characteristics and returned the bottle to On Khotaung rather
ungraciously. That night he drank it up himself with some of his
friends and as a result fell through a hole in the floor of the hut in
which we were both sleeping. The floor was made of split bamboo
and he cut his back and shirt rather badly on the edge of it as he
went through it.

Descending into the Kabaw Valley from Kangpat was like
entering an oven. It was indeed a valley of death in which one saw
neither birds nor animals, but was continually bitten by tiny
insects that penetrated an Army issue mosquito net with the
greatest of ease. The Burma border ran down the centre of the
valley roughly along the bed of a river called the Nam Aya which
flows into the Yu River above Tamu. In peacetime there had been
a few Shan villages in the area whose inhabitants had earned a
livelihood from the manufacture of rock salt at Thanan. But for
months it had been a main Japanese line of communication, and
all the Shans had long since gone. Not even the villages remained
to tell the tale. Everywhere one went there were abandoned
enemy vehicles and skeletons and corpses.

For a further week the regular troops were held up by a small
Japanese rearguard on the last range of hills separating the Kabaw
Valley from the Chindwin, and my men and I built ourselves a hut
on the hillside a little above Thanan at a point some distance away
from the stinking area of open latrines and decaying Japanese
bodies that marked the site of the old Japanese staging camp.
There I was joined by an officer new to V Force called Gillett with
whom I moved on to the Chindwin when the enemy at last
withdrew to the east bank.

PART TWO

Upper Chindwin

1

Gillett was a tall thin bespectacled young man who had been brought up as a Quaker. At Cambridge he had been one of the founders of the Socialist Society and obtained a Double First. In civilian life he had been a schoolmaster. He was undoubtedly the cleverest officer that ever served in V Force but his methods of working were so very different from my own that we were a badly suited combination.

When we reached the Kabaw Valley the Kuki and Naga levies seemed unwilling to accompany us any further and it became imperative that we should establish some sort of contact with the Shans who lived along the banks of the Upper Chindwin River on the other side of the range. At the time of the initial enemy crossings of the river these had been notoriously treacherous to the British, and although in the camp at Thanan we had hoped against hope that some of them would come through the lines to establish contact with us we were disappointed. Perhaps the Shans in the Tonnhe—Thaungdut area had seen a little too much of the war to feel any confidence in the ultimate victory of either side. They had seen the early skirmishes along the river bank between V Force and the Japanese irregular forces under the Hikari Kikan just after the retreat from Burma. They had seen Wingate's First Chindit columns move east into the area of the Irrawaddy and in the fullness of time they had seen the remnants return in the last stages of exhaustion harassed mercilessly by the enemy at every point. At that time it must indeed have seemed that the Japanese were likely to win the war. But when they had advanced into Manipur the same Shan villagers had seen them driven back in their turn starving and exhausted.

While we were held up by the enemy rearguards in the mountains above Thanan, Gillett, who invariably thought further ahead than I, evolved grandiose plans as to how we should contact the representatives of the Burmese trade union movement in Thaungdut and use them to form the basis of a Shan intelligence organisation on the east bank of the river. I was tempted to remind him of these plans when we eventually reached the Thaungdut area, but refrained. The village, like all the others along the river bank in that area, was a ruin and nowhere was there a single Shan to be seen. If there ever had been a Burmese trade union organisation in the Upper Chindwin area it had certainly disintegrated during the course of the war.

During the advance from Manwunjang I had been obliged to leave small parties of Assam Riflemen at various points along the route guarding dumps of rations and stores that it had been impossible to carry forward with us. A large number of the Kuki and Naga scouts in the mountains had been unpaid for more than two months, and in view of the war being unlikely ever to return into the Manipur Hills the problem of disbanding them or at any rate reducing the numbers that we were to keep employed seemed a matter of the first importance. There had moreover been a big reorganisation of Assam Zone V Force and I learned that my sub-area was in future to come under the command of Colonel Stanley of 2 V Ops. It seemed essential that I should return to Kangpat and the hill country for two days to close down the V Force organisation in that area and establish contact with Colonel Stanley who was, I understood, in the hills somewhere to the north. Until the end of the monsoon there was no suggestion of advancing beyond the Chindwin River, so I left Gillett at Tonnhe and returned across the range having sent runners ahead of me to summon a meeting of headmen and V Force leaders at Kangpat.

The meeting was a very difficult one. Now that the war had passed on the tribesmen were reluctant to see V Force disbanded and their weapons taken away from them. Most of them, particularly the less reliable among them, were anxious to be given testimonials. There was moreover not enough money to pay off all concerned. I did what I could to satisfy as many people as possible

SKETCHMAP OF THAUNGDUT AREA

(Scale: 1 Inch to 15 Miles.)

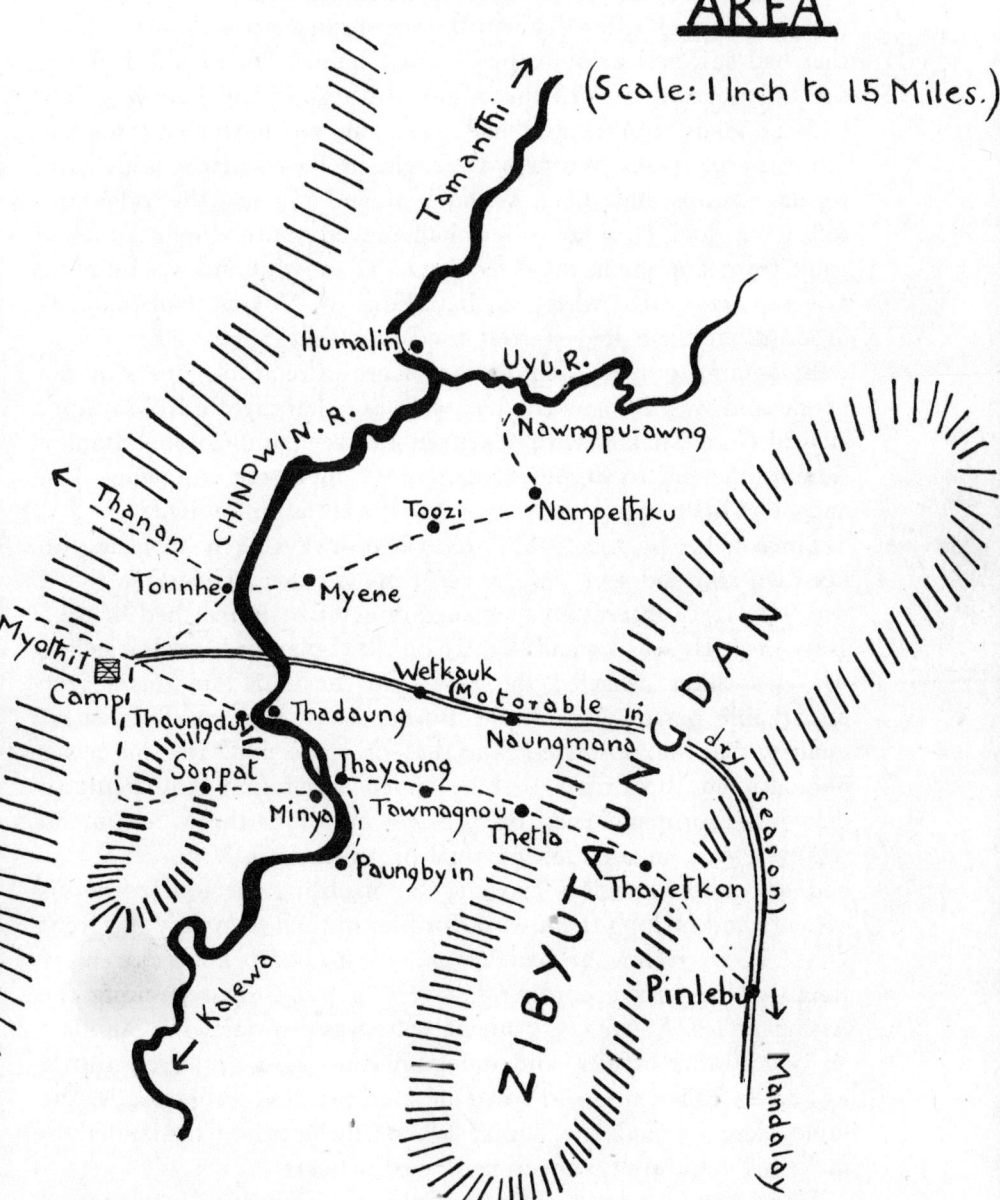

and made careful notes of the grievances of all the others for transmission to higher authority, and closed in the rear parties of Assam Riflemen after distributing the surplus rice to those villages that had suffered most at the Japanese hands. Then I set off down the hill once more into the oppressive heat of the Kabaw Valley with as many coolies as I had been able to muster carrying the more useful stores. We slept the night in Thanan from which the regular troops had been withdrawn and crossed the ridge the following day. I found Gillett had moved south down the river bank from Tonnhe in the direction of Thaungdut and was building a camp close to where a battalion of Dogras had had its headquarters. He had started to contact the Shan villagers who were coming out of their hiding places in remote corners of the jungle and was doing extremely well. But that night a Kuki runner arrived from Thanan with a written message from Colonel Stanley summoning me to attend a conference there the following day, and I had little opportunity to study the situation in detail.

Since being posted to V Force I had always been operating on my own and had seen very little of my brother officers, so that I was extremely interested to meet Stanley of whom I had heard a great deal. He was a small slightly built tea planter from Darjeeling who was later awarded the DSO and the OBE and was a very remarkable personality on the Burma front. Perhaps the greatest quality that he possessed was that of leadership. He was never dogmatic in the orders that he issued and found it difficult to deliver a reprimand even on the few occasions that a reprimand was necessary in such an informal organisation as V Force, but he had an almost magical capacity for inspiring the loyalty of his officers and making them work for him in their own very different ways. In Darjeeling he had learned to speak Gurkhali extremely fluently and was accordingly a very popular figure among the Assam Rifles. Above everything else he was obviously first and last an operational officer, and indeed he invariably appeared a little lost when called upon to solve an administrative problem. At the same time he had the ability when the occasion demanded to make his mark upon a meeting of staff officers.

I had brought back with me from the Chindwin a packet of Burmese cheroots and he had appeared with my liquor ration for the month so that we had quite a convivial party in the old camp above the Japanese cemetery. He had brought me a new wireless set and generator and two Gurkha wireless operators to replace the Anglo-Burmese from the Burma Signals that I had had with me from 3 V Ops. In addition he was accompanied by a fresh platoon of Assam Riflemen from the 3rd Battalion of the Assam Rifles which was to relieve the men from the 4th Battalion who had been with me up till then. It was commanded by a very impressive looking Thapa Jemedar called Hin Bahadur. For the first time since I had left Imphal two months before I learned details of the war.

During the siege the only V Force sub-area that had been able to operate in the way that sub-areas usually operated had been my own. All the other officers had been engaged in the much more dangerous business of close patrolling under the command of regular infantry brigades all round the mountain perimeter. Now that the Japanese had withdrawn to the east bank of the Chindwin River 2 V Ops was to form an intelligence screen along the west bank while the regular troops were to be withdrawn to Imphal. Until the close of the monsoon there were to be no further offensive operations against the enemy, except for the East Africans who were to push south down the Kabaw Valley to the Chin Hills and Kalewa. 3 V Ops were to work in support of them doing flank reconnaissance. Stanley had most of his officers still far away to the north at Kohima and in the Somra Tract, but in the course of the next few weeks he intended to move them south into positions on either side of me along the river bank. In the meantime Gillett and I were to start building up an intelligence organisation across the river. To the north east General Stilwell's American trained Chinese and Wingate's Special Force were pushing south along the railway from Myitkyina and in the gap between the two armies there were some Kachin levies operating under command of the American OSS.

The next day I returned to Gillett's camp above Thaungdut leaving the Jemedar behind with a rear party at Thanan. The sub-area that Colonel Stanley had allotted to me stretched along the bank of the Chindwin River from Thaungdut in the south to a little jungle village called Tabaw in the north, a distance of about six miles. This was the area in which the Japanese had made their first crossings and from which they had finally evacuated the west bank of the river and it showed all the ravages of war. Most of the villages had been burned to the ground and the Shans' rice stocks plundered. Even the cattle had been killed off and there seemed little likelihood of the fields being cultivated that year. Thaungdut had formerly been the capital of a small independent Shan State ruled over by a native *Sawba*, but this worthy had thrown in his lot with the enemy and evacuated with the royal wives and elephants to the east bank early in the campaign. The palace in which he had once lived was a ruin.

During my absence Gillett had started to construct a camp in the jungle in the hills above Thaungdut close to the main track leading west over the range to Myothit in the Kabaw Valley. Each morning he walked down the track for about a mile in the direction of the river to a small bamboo hut where he interviewed any local people who chose to visit him. There he would spend the day stripped to the waist looking rather like a benign old missionary, questioning new arrivals searchingly and making copious notes of their answers.

One of the difficulties that we had faced as we approached the Chindwin had been that we had no one with us who spoke Burmese. During my absence Gillett had overcome this by discovering a very seedy and derelict youth called Tontin who described himself as an Anglo-Burmese and spoke English, Burmese and a little Hindustani. He was not an attractive personality and eventually we discovered that he was in reality an Indo-Burmese who had come up into the area with the Japanese forces from Central Burma and worked with them as an interpreter as far as Ukhrul. This information did not serve to enhance my opinion of him, but I saw the force of Gillett's argument that any interpreter was better than none.

One morning when we were down at the little hut I noticed a short bandy-legged figure dressed in a white woollen smock of the pattern worn by Kukis standing on the outskirts of the crowd of Shans that was assembled. Catching his eye I moved quietly over towards him. As I approached he came to attention and greeted me in Gurkhali.

'Who are you?' I asked.

'My name's Sanschak. I'm a Haukip Kuki.'

'What are you doing in this country?'

'I settled here before the war.'

'Where d'you live?'

'In Sanpat.'

I searched carefully on the map but found no trace of a village of that name. A little further south, however, in the hills behind Minya a Sanpat Chaung was marked. On further questioning it appeared that there was a small Kuki village of six houses called after the *chaung* hidden away in the jungle in that area. The Japs had never visited it during the occupation. Telling Sanschak to go over and get himself a mess tin of tea from the Assam Riflemen that we had with us, I returned to sit by Gillett and sent for one of the few Kuki scouts from Manipur that remained with our party. When he came I asked him what he knew of Sanschak.

'He was at one time in the 4th Battalion, but he finished his time and settled in Burma.'

'Is he a good man?'

'Before the Japs came he was a good man, sahib. Now who can tell!'

'Listen,' I said to him, 'we're going to walk down with him to the village at the foot of the hill and have a talk to him on the way. Afterwards I want you to tell me whether you think he's all right. If you say he is, I'm going to use him as my personal interpreter.'

The Kuki nodded. I lit a pipe, said good-bye to Gillett and set off with the two of them down the hill. At the foot of it the track crossed a stream that was flowing too high for us to wade across, so we settled ourselves on a tree trunk that was lying on the ground and I lit my pipe and gave both the Kukis cigarettes.

'Have you been across the Chindwin since the Japs went?' I asked Sanschak.

'No, sahib.'

'Are there any Japs on the opposite bank?'

'No, sahib.'

'How do you know there are no Japs on the opposite bank?'

Sanschak grinned.

'If I go across the river, will you come with me?'

'If you order me to, sahib.'

All at once I made up my mind. The man was probably a rascal in the way that most border Kukis were, but he had been a soldier and I needed a personal interpreter and I liked the look of him so much better than Tontin.

'Can you speak Shan?' I asked him.

'Yes, sahib.'

'Listen,' I said, 'I need a man who can speak Shan and come round the villages with me to translate. If I give you a gun and pay you, will you work for me?'

For a moment Sanschak was hesitant. He had been out of the Army for four years and he had a wife in Sanpat, but I think that he wanted to be involved in the war. Finally he said that he would have to go back to his village and talk to his wife, and that he would return to my camp in two days' time.

When I returned to the hut Gillett was having a discussion with a tall well-built Shan who had worked for the civil authorities in some capacity or other. He was saying through the medium of Tontin that when the Japs had withdrawn to the other side of the river they had left behind them about a dozen elephants that had originally been brought from Central Burma to carry supplies across the Tonnhe–Thanan track. These were making themselves a sore nuisance to the neighbourhood by eating the fruit on the trees and trampling down crops in the few fields that were under cultivation. I had had nothing to do with elephants previously and I was a little at a loss as to what to suggest. But one of the Havildars in the Assam Rifles called Priti Prasad Limbu appeared to be very knowledgeable on the subject. At his suggestion I told the Shan to collect some of the likelier young men in the area for the purpose of catching the elephants and bringing them up to the camp. This answer seemed to satisfy all concerned and I felt it unlikely that we should hear any more about the matter.

Gillett had been compiling a list of the number of boats in the various villages along the river bank. Most of them had been removed by the Japanese at the time of their withdrawal but there were still one or two very small ones that had been hidden in various places along the river bank. Later that day the headman of

Tabaw came in to visit us for the first time. I did not know then, but I was told later, that he had been one of the few Shan headmen who had been entirely loyal to the British cause even when the Japanese invasion force was living in the villages along the opposite bank prior to crossing into Manipur. He had a brother who was headman of a village on the other side of the river who had the reputation of being hand in glove with the enemy. The official V Force theory concerning this was that the two of them had put their heads together as soon as it became evident that their area was to become a battlefield and decided that the best way to ensure the ultimate well-being of their family was to have an interest in both camps. Accordingly the Tabaw headman had supported the British and his brother the Japanese.

To begin with it must have seemed that the Tabaw headman had had very much the worst of the bargain, but he had continued to give our patrols his wholehearted support. He brought us that day the useful information that he had two large dug-out canoes hidden close by his village and was in a position to ferry our patrols across the river at any time. He said that he had had no contact with the east bank of the river since the enemy had withdrawn, largely because the boatmen were afraid of being shot up by the RAF in midstream, but that it was generally believed that they had withdrawn east from the river bank to beyond the first range of hills, a distance of ten miles away.

At that time neither Gillett nor I knew of his reputation as a loyalist, but we both liked the look of him and before he departed we presented him with a small bag of salt, a rare luxury in that part of Burma at that time.

2

Behind the V Force camp and a little further up the ridge there was a battalion of Dogras in position. They were new arrivals on the Burma front, and had been sent out from Imphal to relieve the previous column when it withdrew. Their forward company, commanded by a stocky red-haired major called Desmond Walker who had come out to India on the same ship as I had, was bivouacing slightly ahead of the battalion and close to us. Every evening he and Gillett had been feeding together. His battalion had taken an air drop recently on a stretch of hillside that they had cleared for the purpose and we were drawing rations from them until such time as we should start to receive air drops of our own.

Desmond Walker had been a hockey blue at Oxford and was a schoolmaster in civilian life. It was pleasant after the lonely weeks that I had spent in the mountains since Pip Fraser-Smith's departure to sit late into the night over a bottle of rum talking with people who spoke the same language as oneself.

That night after Desmond went off to bed Gillett and I held a council of war. Colonel Stanley had ordered me not to cross the Chindwin until further orders lest the presence of a British officer on the other side might cause the Japs to reinforce areas of the bank which the generals in Imphal did not wish them to reinforce. But our next main task would obviously be to develop intelligence sources on the other side and so far none of the villagers seemed to have come across to the west bank. The Thaungdut and Tonnhe area was not very interesting in itself as it had been the scene of the final Japanese evacuation and was badly ravaged. But all the villagers were speaking of a village called Minya about two days' march to the south on the west bank where there were apparently still large stocks of rice available and we therefore decided that I should visit the place as soon as Sanschak returned. While I was away Gillett would continue to build up an intelligence organisation in the Thaungdut area and attempt to induce some of the villagers to cross the river and bring us back information from the other side. The Gurkhas were to set about building a permanent camp. In the Manipur hills there had been very little bamboo, which is the ideal building material in the jungle, but in the mountains on that side of the Kabaw Valley there was a great deal of it.

Next day we received a message from Stanley informing us that a Spitfire pilot had been seen to crash-land in the jungle on the opposite side of the river. I had not yet been down to the river bank but I had heard that the water was running very high and was over four hundred yards across. I told Tontin to write out a message in Burmese to the headmen of the villages along the bank telling them to look out for the pilot and to bring him to our camp if he should appear. But in my own mind I decided that his chances of survival were very slight.

Sanschak came into the camp about midday. He had with him another Kuki from a little village in the neighbourhood and his small son aged ten. The Kukis in this village were starving and they were anxious to send the man and his son along with my party to Minya in the hope that I might use my influence to persuade the Shans to sell them some rice. I felt rather sorry for the Kuki minority in the Chindwin Valley and enlisted the man and his son in V Force.

When Sanschak had passed Gillett's reception post on the way up the hill Gillett had given him a message for me. Apparently the Shan Villagers had brought up fourteen elephants that had been collected along the west bank of the river after the Japanese withdrawal. I hastily seized my hat and my big Colt automatic and set off down the track towards the river. As I left camp I saw the knowledgeable Havildar Priti Prasad Limbu drinking a cup of tea in one of the little shelters that we had erected against the rain and I told him to come with me.

Outside the meeting place thirteen very large elephants and one baby elephant had been drawn up in a line. In and around them an animated crowd of young Shans were shouting and arguing and adjusting howdahs made of creeper. In front stood the tall ascetic figure of Gillett, bare to the waist, holding a laboured conversation through the medium of Tontin with a village dignitary, who appeared to be in charge of the elephants. Tontin was being particularly listless in his role of interpreter that morning.

'The man says that one of the elephants is a bad elephant and that you must shoot it,' he was saying.

'How d'you mean a bad elephant?' I asked.

'It is very savage and angry. If you do not shoot it now, it will make all the other elephants savage and angry.'

'Which is the bad elephant?' I asked.

Tontin walked down the line to a fine big beast munching some leaves a little apart from the others. It looked placid enough to me but the Shans pointed their spears towards it in very dramatic fashion as if it was liable to charge us at any moment. I felt singularly ill-at-ease.

'D'you know how you shoot an elephant?' I asked Gillett rather shiftily.

He seemed to remember that a bullet between the eyes would be lethal, and believed that there was another vulnerable point behind their ears. By way of a second opinion I asked Havildar Priti Prasad. His knowledge of elephants was quite evidently just as theoretical as ours, and he was looking nearly as nervous as I felt myself. He thought that if you fired a bullet into the trunk of an elephant it would at once drop dead. Tontin was grinning at us in a quite infuriating way.

'I don't think I want to start trying to kill elephants unless it's absolutely necessary,' I said to Gillett at last. 'If we postpone matters for a few days while we send back a message to the civil authorities asking for instructions, we may in the end find that it is quite unnecessary to kill it.'

Gillett was made of sterner stuff than I was and his scientific interest had been awakened. He thought that if we trained three Bren guns on the beast it would not matter very much where we hit it as the poor beast would be practically cut to pieces. I was, however, adamant. I pointed out that it would first be necessary to separate the rogue elephant from the others in order to avoid a stampede when we opened fire and that it would be wise to refer the matter to Colonel Stanley, who, as an old tea planter, would probably know exactly how such an execution should be carried out. We learned later that there was in reality nothing wrong with

The Chawida headman, Saw San Sein, Padu, the Doctor, Saw Thet Wa, Captain Michael Fielding, myself, and Sergeants Moore and Rowe, with Karen levies

Hyena Area Headquarters on Mount Plakho

The Lysander which brought Fielding in before take-off from Rangoon

Saw San Sein, myself, Saw Thet Wa, Moore, the Doctor and Rowe with three Mobile Levies

this particular elephant. The local Shans were very short of meat and they hoped by inducing us to shoot it to provide themselves with a generous supply for many days to come.

I left for Minya the following day with Sanschak and the two other Kukis and fourteen Gurkhas. The rains had been falling off during the past fortnight and the level of the *chaung* which crossed the track at the foot of the mountains had fallen about six feet, so that we were able to wade across it with the water never reaching above our waists.

Up till that time I had seen very little of the Chindwin Valley proper. The villages, such as Tonnhe, through which I had passed, had been largely destroyed during the Japanese invasion and their inhabitants were living in hide-outs in the jungle. But south of the Thaungdut Chaung my little column passed into a narrow valley into which the enemy had never penetrated in large numbers.

Coming out of the rugged fastnesses of the Manipur hills and the poisonous foetid atmosphere of the Kabaw Valley it was like entering an exotic and slightly decadent fairyland from which a more sinister realm of hobgoblins and evil yellow dwarfs was never very far away. The people wore brightly coloured clothes and their houses were airy and clean. The girls were pretty and subtly aware of their own charms. No one ever seemed to be working very hard and even the small children smoked enormous cheroots.

I had already met a number of the inhabitants who had been up to the V Force camp to meet either Gillett or me, and I was continually greeted by acquaintances at each village that we passed through. In their approach to us the Shans were invariably courteous and dignified, and there was none of the subservience that one meets with so often in India. I decided that I liked these people, even though they had been a very treacherous element during the Japanese occupation.

At one village a strange wizened-looking young man wearing a blue pork-pie hat greeted me in English. Rather surprised, I took the opportunity of calling a halt and he invited me into his house where we drank tea without milk out of little round cups with no handles. He told me his name was Tabi and embarked on a long account of how helpful he had been to the survivors of Wingate's

First Chindit expedition who had passed through Thaungdut in their escape. This approach made me a little suspicious, but English-speaking Shans were extremely valuable as interpreters and I looked sympathetic. He had been educated at a Baptist Mission School at Mawlaik where he had learned English and retained his Buddhist beliefs. Before the war he had been a trader in Burmese cheroots and patent medicines in Thaungdut, but his house had been destroyed by bombers during the invasion and he had evacuated to this obscure backwoods village with his mother, wife and child.

When I rose to make my departure his face took on a very serious expression and his English seemed to fail him in his anxiety.

'You have medicine?' he asked.

'What sort of medicine?'

'My stomach. It is no good. I have always soft faeces now.'

I gave him some chalk and opium tablets and told him to come and see me at my camp in a week's time. Then we continued on our way. Shortly after leaving the village Sanschak led us out of the narrow valley and up into a range of low hills to the east between the main ridge and the Chindwin River. For a while we followed the bed of a small mountain stream until it became little more than a tiny trickle around our ankles and then after a short steep stretch through thick bamboo we reached the crest of the hill from which we caught a distant glimpse of the Chindwin River through the trees. Then the path descended into a ravine through which the Sanpat Chaung flowed. We crossed it at a point where the water ran knee deep and then, tired and content, we arrived in Sanpat village where a delegation of Kukis awaited us with bottles of *zoo* in their hands.

We slept the night in a hut which had been cleared for us in the village and next day moved on to Minya in almost torrential rain. Crossing a *jume* field where another Kuki family was living in a small hut the track wound through thick jungle for about eight hundred yards. Beneath our boots the surface of the ground had degenerated into slimy evil-smelling mud into which we sank as far as our ankles. Then very suddenly we reached the shore of a large inland lake across which we could see in the distance about a mile away the pagodas and monasteries at Minya rising above the trees. Evidently our arrival was not unexpected for a fleet of dug-out canoes manned by Shan villagers was awaiting us. In these we were paddled across the lake to the village.

On the surface Minya was a very ordinary village, but in the atmosphere there was something that made one feel uneasy. Unlike all the other villages in the area it did not appear to suffer from any ill effects as a result of the Japanese occupation. In the fields there was a fresh rice crop coming up and there were cattle and water buffaloes grazing quite openly wherever there was grass. Chickens and ducks abounded and women were pounding paddy on the clumsy wooden machines that the Shans use for the purpose.

It was a big village and was divided into three separate groups of houses stretching for more than a mile along the river bank. The centremost of these was Minya proper and gave its name to the whole area. The *thugyi* of the northernmost group of houses appeared to be a friend of Sanschak and had come in the boats to fetch us. It was to his house that we were taken after our arrival and treated to an enormous meal of chicken and rice and boiled eggs followed by bananas and Shan tea and Burmese cheroots. The Gurkhas' faces started to brighten very considerably after their long march in the rain. I decided that the inhabitants of Minya must have very guilty consciences indeed. But I made myself as affable as possible and carried on a very halting conversation with the headman in Burmese, which I had been studying daily since we had crossed the border. He was hugely amused by my linguistic efforts.

After the meal I took a walk down the river front with Sanschak. Opposite Minya on the other side of the river there is a village called Thayaung. The river at that point is nearly half a mile wide in the monsoon, and it was impossible to see the other bank very clearly in the rain. But I noticed that there were dug-out canoes tied up on both banks. I addressed the *thugyi* in my best Burmese, which I could never make to sound very spontaneous.

'*Yandhu ho ywa hma shi-de-la?*' (Are there any enemy in that village?)

He gave me for reply the inevitable '*Mishibu*' which must be the most frequent word in the Burmese language and has a dozen different meanings all of which signify absence.

'Do you not cross in the boats?'

'No, *thakin.*'

'Why?'

'We are afraid.'

I did not believe him, but I said nothing.

While we were talking, the *thugyi* of Minya appeared carrying a large unbrella and followed by a long retinue of elders. He was a little rat-faced shifty-eyed fellow of middle age, who created rather a sinister impression. He was quite evidently terrified of me. My party was invited along to his house where we were entertained to a second banquet more opulent than the last.

After I had eaten I thought long on the situation over a series of Burmese cheroots. I decided that the reason why Minya had not suffered during the invasion to the same extent as the other villages was probably because it had been more frankly collaborationist. It had probably been the site of a large enemy headquarters which had restrained the retreating Imperial infantry to a great extent from plunder and depredations. At the same time it seemed only too clear that the main source of intelligence for the area would be at Minya rather than at Thaungdut. In the former village there was rice and consequently it would be a rallying point for the whole neighbourhood. There would be gossip and intrigue and an ideal background for both enemy agents and our own. I decided that until such time as one of Colonel Stanley's other officers came into position at Minya from the north I would be advised to concentrate on the area in preference to my own.

That night I made a small informal speech to the headmen and *lugyis*, which Sanschak translated. I thanked them for their hospitality and explained that the Japanese had left north Burma and that they would never see them again. I told them that soon there would be another British officer coming to the area to organise them and work in their midst. But that in the meantime they were to send any information that they might obtain from across the Chindwin up to the camp at Thaungdut. I tried to appear friendly, but at the same time to convey the impression that I would be extremely unpleasant if I was crossed.

In the morning Sanschak's friend the headman of Minya—North End suggested that we might like to make the return journey to Thaungdut by boat. The weather had changed overnight and it was a beautiful sunny day with hardly a cloud in the sky. So I agreed readily enough. Four large dug-out canoes were allotted to us and, well-fed and burdened with many presents, we set out in these about ten o'clock, hugging the west bank all the time. I smoked innumerable Burmese cheroots and felt at peace with the world. In between times I practised my Burmese on the boatmen. In all the villages along the bank there were girls fishing by the side of the river, standing up to their waists in water and scooping with bamboo baskets for a tiny silver fish not unlike a sardine in appearance. As we passed there was much verbal byplay between them and the Gurkhas.

Towards three o'clock in the afternoon we were approaching the sharp bend in the Chindwin that lies below Thaungdut. As the crow flies we must have been within two miles of the town itself, but on the river we were still an appreciable distance away. In the bend the water narrows between high cliffs into a swirling torrent. As we crept along the west bank I could feel the canoe start to rock. The Shan boatmen were evidently holding a conference, and we seemed to be making little headway. Finally one of them addressed Sanschak.

'What do they say?' I asked.

'They say that if we are to go on we must cross to the other side of the river where the water is calmer than here. On this side the boat will overturn.'

'But what if there are Japs on the other side?'

My query was passed on to the boatmen and my ear caught the inevitable '*Japan mishibu*'.

'Tell them they can cross to the other bank,' I said, and promptly was assailed with the gravest doubts as to the wisdom of the order. But once given I felt that it could not be counter-manded.

The boats turned out into midstream and made for the opposite bank. Around me the Gurkhas sat rigid like frightened statues in stone. Being all of them born and bred in mountain country, where water takes either the form of a trickle on the

hillside or a terrifying mountain torrent, none of them had learned
to swim. To quieten my own misgivings I lit another cheroot. For
a while we were in midstream and both banks were equidistant,
and then very gradually we drew towards the trees on the other
side. My fears were slowly lulled, until at last we reached a point
when I felt that if there were indeed enemy marksmen on the far
bank they would certainly have already opened fire. The leading
boat was not more than twenty yards from the shore when a khaki
clad figure in a peaked cap appeared from out of the bushes. The
Gurkhas still sat like rocks, but their faces grew tenser still. I
decided quickly that this was the end and that it was all my fault.
Only Sanschak gripped his rifle and started to pull back the bolt
with a movement that nearly overturned the boat. But the figure
on the bank was waving a white handerkerchief and yelling wildly:
'American, American.' We had run into the leading patrol of
Stilwell's American guerillas.

As we clambered ashore I was surrounded by a group of short
stocky Kachins in American battledress. Then came a tall
pompous Shan in a European style felt hat, white shirt and
flowered *lungyi* and a Gurkha who had once served in the Assam
Rifles before he was taken a prisoner of war by the Japanese.
There was a babble of different languages. Shan, Burmese, Hindi,
Gurkhali and English. Everyone was shaking hands, and offering
one another cigarettes. One little Kachin who spoke Hindi kept on
asking me if I had seen the 2nd Battalion.

'The 2nd Battalion of what?' I said at last.

'The 2nd Burma Rifles. I lost them in the retreat.'

I told him that as far as I knew the remnants of the Burma
Army were several thousand miles away at Hoshiarpur in the
Punjab, and he looked very disappointed. He had been expecting
them in the van. Finally the Gurkha took charge of the situation.
He explained to me that he was a section commander in a force of
American levies working from Nawngpuawng about two days'
march to the north and had been ordered to patrol as far south as
Thayaung down the east bank of the river. He told me his officer
was an American who went by the name of Greek. I wrote out a
short message to Greek telling him our dispositions on the west
bank and then we took our farewells and re-embarked. For

another hour we crept up the east bank of the river safe in the knowledge that the area had been patrolled by the American guerillas and then when the river widened again beyond the bend we crossed to Thaungdut. By that time darkness was closing in, so I called a halt in the first village that we came to and we slept the night in a large comfortable Shan house. At dawn we moved on to the camp above Thaungdut.

While I had been away the Dogra Regiment had had orders to withdraw to Imphal. Just before they had marched off some of the Shan villagers had brought in the Spitfire pilot who had crash-landed on the other side of the Chindwin. He was a young Australian sergeant and had had a very trying march home. As much by luck as by good judgment he had managed to crash-land his plane in some elephant grass about six miles east of the river. Without any delay he had grabbed his maps and a revolver and fled into the jungle. Within two minutes of the landing he had heard voices which he believed to be Japanese in the neighbourhood of the aeroplane. Avoiding all paths he had set off in a westerly direction towards the Chindwin. In that area cross-country movement was difficult enough for an infantryman, and for a pilot with little or no jungle training his march must have been an exhausting experience.

After three days he reached the river bank. He had carried with him only sufficient rations for one day and was by that time extremely hungry. After dark he stripped down into a pair of shorts and set out to swim the river. But after getting out a hundred yards into midstream he had turned back realizing that the current was too strong, and that he would never make the opposite bank. The force of the current had carried him a considerable distance down-stream by that time and he was unable to find his way back to the place where he had left his clothes. There were a great many mosquitoes on the river bank and he had been bitten badly during the night. By morning he was suffering acutely from hunger and exhaustion, but he had nevertheless kept going down the river bank in the hope that he might eventually come across a boat.

After midday his efforts were rewarded, when he came upon an abandoned Japanese supply dump in which among many other

items of equipment there had been a number of collapsible rubber
dinghies and a device for blowing them up. Again he had waited
until nightfall before making his second attempt to cross. This
time he had been successful and he had landed at a Shan village
south of Thaungdut where the villagers had seemed friendly. The
following day they had taken him up to Gillett's camp.

Before the Dogras left they had received on their dropping zone
a goodwill sortie of rice for the local villagers, and while I was
away Gillett had distributed this very efficiently to the various
headmen who seemed to be in the greatest need. The Civil
Government were very jealous of their rights in such matters and
were continually sending in complaints about the activities of
V Force in the forward areas, but as they seldom left the safety of
the large headquarters themselves they were very ineffective.

Gillett felt rather more competitive about the advance of the
Americans that I did. He was fresh from Imphal and anxious to be
ahead of our allies in the advance if it could be possibly contrived.
As luck would have it the wireless generator had broken down and
we were out of communication with Colonel Stanley's headquarters in Nambashi except by runner. In my absence Gillett had,
however, received a message asking him to confirm a report from
civilian government sources that there was a brigade of Japs in
position on the east bank of the Chindwin opposite Thaungdut. It
was a convincing sort of report giving the name of the regiment
and other details.

'It can't be true,' I said, 'I crossed very close to that point last
night and should almost certainly have been fired on if there had
been any one there. And in any case the American patrol must
have walked right through the place.'

'Well, at any rate it's a good excuse for me to ignore the ban on
crossing the Chindwin and go and see,' said Gillett.

I laughed, and it was agreed that he should cross the river the
following day on a four-day patrol on the east bank. That morning
I wrote out a long written report to Colonel Stanley which I sent
off by runner to Nambashi by two Kukis who had come in with
messages the previous day. Then I went and reviled the wireless
operators for allowing the petrol generator to break down. Gillett
had gone down to the river with a pair of binoculars to see what

was to be seen across the river. I had a long luxurious bath in the stream and settled down to sew a few buttons on to my trousers. At about tea-time Tabi, the English-speaking Shan from Thaungdut, arrived, and while I was talking to him we heard aeroplanes overhead. They were fighters and we counted twelve of them flying east.

'That means a bit of trouble for the Jap,' I remarked to Tabi, and just as I spoke we saw them dive towards the Chindwin and we could hear their guns going. About an hour later Gillett arrived back in camp. He had been in a canoe in the Thaungdut *chaung*, when an air strike had taken place in the village on the opposite side of the Chindwin, and had been terrified lest the fighters should turn their attentions to him after they had finished. They had evidently been strafing the supposed position of the Japanese brigade.

The following day Gillett crossed the Chindwin with Havildar Priti Prasad and six Assam Riflemen and a Burmese-speaking Naga who had come with us all the way from Nambashi. Everything was very quiet while he was away. Every morning I went down to the little hut at the foot of the mountains to interview anyone who chose to come up and see me. No one brought any information about the enemy and finally I came to believe that these must indeed have withdrawn some distance inland from the east bank.

Then on the day Gillett was due to return Colonel Stanley appeared from the south with a platoon of Gurkhas that he was sending to Sanpat to await the arrival of Tibbetts, another of his officers. The platoon commander was a cheerful looking little Jemedar who had won the MC at the siege of Kohima. Colonel Stanley was never happier than when away from the atmosphere of headquarters and we spent a pleasant hour trying out a new American carbine that he had been given by a brigade of the Special Force with which he had worked in the Somra Tract. He had originally intended to cross the range to Myothit the same day, but he changed his plans when he heard that Gillett was due in from patrol that evening, as he was anxious to take back any information with him and in any case intended sending Gillett off to open up a new sub-area south of the East Africans who had advanced from Tamu as far as the Chindwin at Sittaung, and wished to meet him before he went.

Gillett came in about five o'clock having made a very useful
patrol. He had crossed the river opposite the point which had been
straffed by the RAF and confirmed that the enemy had left the
place three weeks before. Two Shan women had been killed in the
airstrike and local feeling had been somewhat antagonised by the
incident. South of that village he had come upon what was
evidently the main Japanese approach route to the Chindwin from
the Irrawaddy, which debouched onto the river bank opposite
Thaungdut. This must have been a good motorable track in the
dry season, but it was then deep in mud and vehicles of all
descriptions were bogged at intervals all along it. He had followed
it for two days, counting 132 abandoned motor vehicles in the
process and finally reaching a village called Wetkauk where he had
turned back. Everywhere the villagers told him that the Japs had
gone. They all seemed ready to be friendly, but in a rather
apathetic sort of way. There was a great shortage of rice
throughout the area.

Before leaving Nambashi Stanley had given orders for his
headquarters to be moved forward into the Kabaw Valley to the
site of a village called Myothit that had been destroyed during the
Japanese invasion. This lay beside the track on the other side of
the mountain to the east. He was therefore delighted to hear of
our elephant train, as these would be invaluable for transporting
stores backwards and forwards until the rains ended in November
and the tracks in the Kabaw Valley became motorable once more.
He left the day after Gillett's return with the animals plodding
slowly along behind him. Even the one that was alleged to be a
rogue had been saddled with an improvised howdah for the
occasion.

Gillett left two days afterwards travelling by boat down the
Chindwin at night and I started preparing for a long range patrol
across the river. Sanschak had departed to his village for a few
days' leave while Gillett had been on the other side of the river.
After he returned I held a long conference with him and the
headman of Tabaw and a tall thick set villager called Chu Deh
from Dokthida on the east bank of the river who had agreed to act

as one of my agents. During the Japanese invasion the *Kempei Tai* (secret police) had imposed a very rigid control over all travellers. No villager had been allowed to move more than a day's journey from his own home without a pass. These passes were difficult to come by and it was seldom worth anyone's while to apply for one. The memory of those restrictions was fresh in the minds of the Shans and all of them seemed reluctant to circulate far from their homes.

Nevertheless it seemed certain as a result of Gillett's patrol to Wetkauk that the enemy had withdrawn some distance east from the river bank. My inability to pinpoint their advanced positions irritated me intensely, and I decided that this time I would go out for ten days and proceed as far as the Zibyutaungdan which was a range of hills running north to south parallel to the Chindwin River and about thirty miles to the east. On the map it stood out as the next obvious defensive line along which the enemy might take up a position. And there I felt there were sure to be enemy posts.

The great difficulty would be rations. It was impractical to expect my men to carry more than four days' rations in their packs without so weighing themselves down as to lose all mobility. Most of them had been continuously on operations of one sort or another since the enemy had first advanced into Manipur over six months before and during the monsoon their stamina had been taxed to breaking point. Malaria and jungle sores were rife amongst us, and it was months since we had seen any fresh vegetables. On the other hand it would be quite impossible to live on the countryside, for throughout the invasion this had been the area through which the main Japanese lines of communication had passed, and the villages had been plundered bare.

I considered the possibility of taking porters with us at any rate as far as Wetkauk. But Tontin insisted that all the villagers were far too weak and undernourished to carry normal loads for any distance. Finally a compromise was effected by which it was decided that we should rely on coolies to carry forward two large sacks of rice from village to village as far as Wetkauk where we would establish a small dump. Thence we would move forward to a village called Sinlamaung at the foot of the Zibyutaungdan where it was hoped that we might get news of the enemy.

I crossed the river shortly after dawn, having warned Stanley by runner so that he could notify the RAF over the wireless, taking with me Sanschak and ten Assam Riflemen comanded by an elderly Havildar from Darjeeling, who amused me immensely. When I had first talked with him he had told me in a melancholy voice that as a boy of twelve in 1914 he had gone down to enlist in the Army and that he had been turned away as too young. Stanley knew his real history. He was an inhabitant of the little independent state of Sikkim to the north of Darjeeling, who came down to the market one day at Tista Bridge on the border, got drunk and found himself in the Army the following morning. He was a loyal hard-working old man but not exactly ideal material for a touch and run raid into enemy territory. With him there was also a fine husky young Lance-Naik called Gawein who I felt would be much more valuable if we met the enemy. He had travelled back with me in the boat from Minya and had been so excited by the spectacle of the Shan girls along the river bank that he had on two occasions very nearly upset the boat. He had a bright eye and a fine thick bull neck.

I also took with me two Shan boys from the west bank whom I had armed with captured Japanese rifles and intended to use as scouts. We spent most of the day in the village which had been so badly strafed by the RAF shortly before, while the two Shan boys moved east in search of information. The villagers seemed rather aloof, but the house of the headman's son was placed at our disposal. He was a tall handsome fellow with an attractive young wife, who flirted with everyone.

At nightfall my scouts came back with the news that no enemy were believed to be in the neighbourhood. At dawn the following day we headed south along the river bank into a teak forest where there was little or no undergrowth and the path wound easily through the trees. The place was a network of abandoned Japanese camps and store dumps, but we had little time to explore it fully. After midday we came out into a broad open rice plain that stretched for miles to the south in the direction of Paungbyin. Here we turned east along a muddy track that crossed a stream innumerable times. The water in it was still high, although the rains were coming to a close, but at every crossing place there was a ferry manned by local boatmen.

Although the Shans were helpful enough, I continued to note a vague suggestion of aloofness and as we moved on across the plain my uneasiness increased. At each village we recruited eight coolies to carry on the two sacks of rice which we had divided into four loads to the next centre of population. For each of these short stages I paid each coolie with a bright silver rupee. Always I kept asking them in Burmese about the enemy, but I could never get a concrete reply. The Japanese were invariably *mishibu*, but no one appeared to know where they really were. But no one else seemed to be the least worried, and I began to wonder whether my nerves were getting bad.

At nightfall we halted in a little Shan village beside the stream that we had been following east ever since we had left the teak forest. It was now only running knee deep when the path passed across it. There were two old Shan ladies and a number of children sleeping in the same house as ourselves, which I felt was a reassuring point. I fed the children with the sweets from an American K ration that I had with me and talked to them in Burmese. They seemed quite happy and unperturbed and told me that the Japanese were very bad people. But I kept double sentries moving around the house throughout the night and I slept in my boots.

In the morning we cooked a rice meal and moved off down the track to the east. The two Shan boys from the west bank were no longer willing to leave our party on lone reconnaissance but they both assured me that they thought the villagers were reliable people. That night I intended to sleep in Wetkauk, the farthest village east that Gillett had visited. The country we moved across was very similar to that through which we had passed the previous day. But at about twelve o'clock we came back onto the motor road constructed by the Japanese and after that every mile or so we would pass an abandoned vehicle. I opened the bonnets of several of these, and found that in each case the rotor arm had been removed but no effort had been made to smash the cylinder heads.

After following the road for another two miles we came

suddenly out into a clearing in which there was a small village, where we seemed to take the only inhabitants, a middle-aged man and two boys by surprise. The man was very surly and unco-operative and I developed an instant dislike for him. When I told him that I wanted eight coolies to take over the loads of rice from a party of the villagers from the place where we had spent the night he told me that there were none available. Sanschak whispered to me that this was a very bad man, a conclusion that I had already reached on my own account, and I dropped the genial benevolent approach to which I generally treated the Shans.

Gawein went and stood by the Shan and said to me in a loud voice that many of his friends had died as a result of Shan treachery and that he believed that the whole lot of them were better dead. The man cannot have understood him but he began to look a little nervous and his truculent manner disappeared. He sent one of the boys to bring coolies.

We had to wait about an hour in the village until they came. The more I saw of the place the more uneasy I felt. There were no women and children in any of the houses, a sure sign that trouble was expected, and yet the man kept on telling me that the Japanese were *mishibu*.

Sanschak was by that time a long way away from Kuki country and not quite as self-confident as he was on the Chindwin River. Then two rather knowing young Shans in gaudy clothes came walking down the track from the east. They said they had come from Sinlamaung, two long days' march distant, and seemed to have no particular reason for coming. I talked to them through Sanschak for a few minutes and then they passed on their way grinning broadly in a very irritating fashion. Shortly afterwards the boy came back with eight young women who were apparently to act as coolies. They were chatting merrily among themselves and were very demure with the Gurkhas, and their presence calmed my anxiety a little.

We set off towards the east. Above us the sun had come out from behind a cloud and we straggled out in a long tired untidy line. Gawein and two Assam Riflemen were moving in front with the aged Havildar, my Chettri orderly, two other Assam Riflemen and I following with the Shan girls. The remainder of the party formed a rear guard. The atmosphere was rather oppressive and we were all very tired. About a mile west of Wetkauk the track passed into some low hills covered with teak jungle where I ordered a short halt. Rather carelessly I neglected to order the party off the track and we all settled ourselves where we had halted and lit our pipes and cigarettes. A pleasant drowsiness came upon me as I puffed away at my pipe. About thirty yards away I could hear the sentry telling Gawein that some American guerillas were coming down the track and I eased myself up onto my elbows.

Then to my gradually awakening consciousness the following rather startling conversation piece penetrated. The sentry shouted out to the newcomers who were evidently as tired as we were: 'Are you Americans?' in Gurkhali, and the reply came back very distinctly and innocently:

'Nippon.'

Gawein started shooting first. The leading Jap received most of a Sten magazine in his stomach at ten yards' range and fell to the ground quietly and without complaint. Behind him there were two more, less badly hit who emitted a strange wailing noise as they fell to the ground. Around me the Shan girls leapt to their feet and disappeared into the bushes. A Jap light machine gun opened up at very close range in front, and I picked up my pack and roared 'Left', setting off up the hill with the Havildar and Sanschak beside me. We halted about a hundred yards up the slope and counted ourselves. A dead silence had closed over the jungle. Everyone was present except two Assam Riflemen who had been at the rear of the party and had disappeared completely. After the repeated assurances that we had received that the enemy were *mishibu* this unexpected encounter had rather taken my breath away.

I consulted my map at some length and saw that there was a track leading north to south about a mile distant to the east which crossed the Wetkauk track. On it there appeared to be an out-of-the-way Shan village, where I decided that we would spend the night and send out villagers to find the two Assam Riflemen that were missing. We headed north-west towards it through the jungle on a rough compass bearing. Such moves are invariably much easier in theory than in practice and it was late in the

afternoon when we reached the village. The headman appeared to
be friendly, and we settled ourselves in his house. Round about
the normal life of the village was going on. Women were cooking
and pounding paddy in the elaborate wooden machines that they
kept for the purpose underneath their houses. Children were
playing happily. I felt that the headman would take good care to
see that we had timely warning of the approach of an enemy. He
had not heard of our skirmish during the afternoon or that there
were any Japs in the neighbourhood.

I posted a double sentry outside the house and we ate a meal of
packed rations that we had with us. I ordered everyone to sleep in
their boots with their arms ready to hand. At about eight o'clock I
stretched myself out on the floor and settled down to sleep. I was
awakened shortly afterwards by Sanschak who had the headman
with him. The headman was looking worried.

'What's the matter?' I asked.

'The *thugyi* says there are now a hundred Japs in the village
where we got the coolies. We surprised three of them there when
we arrived this morning but they ran away and the rest came
later.'

'How far away is the village from here?'

'About two miles.'

'Does the bad Shan know we are here?'

Sanchak talked with the *thugyi* in Shan.

'He thinks he probably does,' said Sanschak.

I thought about the two occasions on which I had tried to
surround Japanese stragglers in Naga villages back in the Manipur
hills. That had been in broad daylight and on neither occasion had
I been very successful. Outside there was a full moon.

'Ask him whether he thinks it is safe for us to sleep the night
here,' I asked.

Again there was a lengthy conversation in Shan.

'He says that it is wiser for you to go. He will provide guides to
the river bank. If the Japs come now there will be much fighting
and women and children may be hurt.'

I called the Havildar and told him to get the men ready to
march. Then I turned again to Sanschak and the headman.

'Somewhere in the jungle two of my Gurkhas are lost. They

must be looked after by the villagers and sent back to my camp at Thaungdut.'

The headman assured me that this would be done. Twenty minutes later, we set out for the Chindwin, very tired and depressed. Two tall well-made Shans lead the way. The path ran through open teak jungle and was fairly level, but the foliage of the trees obscured the light of the moon and our guides were continually losing the track. Their legs were bare but they did not seem frightened of snakes. We marched for five hours and then I ordered a halt when I estimated that we were about three miles from the river bank. I had been checking our direction on my compass throughout the journey in case of treachery. We huddled together in a little circle in the darkness and were badly bitten by mosquitoes, but fortunately it was a dry night.

At dawn we moved on to a village on the river bank from which we could see the ruined pagodas at Tonnhe across the stream to the north-west. There we cooked tea while the headman summoned some boatmen. It was a village that had had a bad reputation in the early days of the war, but the inhabitants seemed friendly enough. We crossed to Tonnhe in two big canoes and went up to the huts in the jungle behind the village where the Shans had gone into hiding during the Japanese occupation. There we slept for two hours and cooked and ate a meal before continuing to the camp above Thaungdut. There I learned that a new charging machine had arrived by elephant the previous day and that we were at last in wireless communication with Colonel Stanley at Myothit. I wrote out a report on the patrol for the signallers to encipher and then went off to sleep.

Our encounter with the Japanese at Wetkauk left me a little shaken. All my information had suggested that the enemy had withdrawn east of the Zibyutaungdan. News travels fast in the jungle and I was convinced that some of the Shans who had told me that the enemy were *mishibu* had been lying. The two missing Assam Riflemen reappeared in camp during the course of the next few days, having been helped on their way home by various groups of villagers. They told a rather terrifying story of hairbreadth escapes, but I discounted a great deal of this as patent exaggeration. Their return removed a considerable weight of anxiety from my mind, but I still remained irritable and depressed. Since my arrival on the Chindwin I had felt that I had gradually won the confidence of the local Shans, and now I knew that they were keeping information from me. As matters had turned out the Japanese had suffered more than we had in the chance encounter, but it might well have been the other way round.

Then one morning Chu Deh, my agent from Dokthida, came across the river with a present of a bunch of bananas. I was drinking tea in the little hut where I recieved visitors each day, and holding concourse with a group of other visitors. He was given a present of a little bag of salt and a mess tin full of tea to drink and retired to squat on the outskirts of the crowd.

These daily gatherings usually dispersed shortly after three o'clock in the afternoon. But that day at four o'clock I noticed that Chu Deh, who had farther to go to his home than any of the others present, was still sitting quite impassively smoking a cheroot. Gradually it dawned on me that he had something he wished to tell me after the others had gone. From previous experience I knew that it would be fatal to rush him in any way, and so I continued a lengthy conversation that I was having with the Gurkhas about nothing in particular. Finally I noticed out of the corner of my eye that Chu Deh was holding a conversation aside with Tontin, but I still pretended to ignore developments and went off down the hill to a point where I practised with my Colt .45 automatic daily. There I fired a few rounds at a tin can. When I returned to the hut the Gurkhas were getting ready to return to camp and of the Shans Chu Deh alone remained. Tontin approached me casually.

'Sir, Chu Deh says there are Japs at Thetla.' Thetla was a village south of Wetkauk and just outside the rice plain lying east of Thayaung.

'How many?' I asked equally casually.

'About fifty. Japs and Shans.'

'When did they go to Thetla?'

'They were left behind there when the others went beyond the Zibyutaungdan.'

'What are they doing there?'

'They are the V Force of Japan.'

I still pretended not to be very interested. I bid Chu Deh a warm farewell and told him to let me know if he heard anything else.

A few days later an ex-Burma Rifleman from the Paungbyin area whom I had met on my first visit to Minya came up to visit me and equally unobtrusively after I had waited half a day for him to speak told me the same thing. As the two of them came from areas far removed from one another I decided that the information was very probably true. The jig-saw puzzle was starting to fit together. The main Japanese rearguard was evidently the other side of the Zibyutaungdan but they had small guerilla intelligence units stationed forward of the hills and one of these was at Thetla. The local Shans were waiting to see which side was going to win the next phase of the war before they gave any active help to either the Japanese or ourselves. We had evidently walked into our Japanese equivalent organisation at Thetla quite by chance.

A number of messages had arrived over the wireless while I had been away. There was to be another reorganisation of the front. The main body of our regular forces was now to push down the Kabaw Valley and into the Chin Hills. Until the capture of Kalewa the spearhead was to be the 11th East African Division. Then after the monsoon the British 2nd Division which was reforming after

the battles around Kohima was to cross the Chindwin and
continue the advance to Mandalay. Imphal was to be held in the
meantime by an independent brigade of six battalions who were
spread out at intervals in positions from which they could cover
the crossings of the Upper Chindwin north of Kalewa. Colonel
Stanley's 2 V Ops was now under command of the Imphal Brigade
and was to concentrate on intelligence from the country east of
the river. A company of the Assam Regiment which was one of
the units of the Imphal Brigade had been moved into my area and
was stationed at a point close to where I normally interviewed
visiting Shans. Later in the day I went down to talk with the
company commander taking Tontin with me. He was a teaplanter
from Southern India who had won the MC at Kohima.

On the way home Tontin started complaining that Jemedar Hin
Bahadur, who was still with the rear party at Thanan, had been
getting into mischief. There was a good deal of surplus rice there
which had been left behind by the various columns of regular
troops that had crossed the ridge and with this he was purchasing
the favours of some of the local village maidens. It was the sort of
episode that would sooner or later lead to trouble, though I was
rather irritated at hearing about it in the first place from Tontin.
That night I sent Hin Bahadur a message ordering him to hand the
rice over to the *thugyi* of Thanan for safe keeping and move his
men forward to my camp.

The next few days passed very quietly with no new information
coming in from across the river. I took an air drop on the dropping
zone that had been cleared by the Dogras in which we received
rum and cigarettes. Then the 2 V Ops doctor arrived from
Myothit. He was a Bengali Hindu called Roy, with a wisp of black
beard on his chin which made him look a little like a Sikh. He
proved to be a very entertaining companion. He had originally
been MO to the Tripura Legion, an ill-starred guerilla expedition
into the Kaladan Valley in the Arakan early in the war, and he had
remained with V Force ever since. I sent him off on a tour of the
villages along the west bank of the Chindwin in my sub-area. The
prospect of medical attention in an area that had been without it
since the Burma retreat three years before was a potent means of
winning the goodwill of the local inhabitants. Before the Japanese

invasion of Manipur there had been an absurd incident, when after a report had been received that a Japanese doctor was inoculating villagers against cholera in Tamanthi, a V Force doctor had proceeded to the same area and in the absence of the requisite serum continued the good work with distilled water. Only in that way had it been possible to maintain prestige.

By that time I realised that I was badly in need of a long rest. It was approaching the middle of October and it had been late in June when I had first left Imphal with Pip Fraser-Smith. Before that I had served for eighteen months without leave as an infantry officer in the Arakan. I was sleeping badly and feeling less and less anxious to cross the Chindwin again. A week had passed since the skirmish at Wetkauk and I decided that the best remedy for my increasing uneasiness was another patrol. The day I made this decision I learned that some American guerillas had occupied Minya. Stanley had had several queries as to exactly what was happening in that area from the Civil Affairs Service personnel with Fourteenth Army, so I decided to go over and secure first hand information for myself, and at the same time cross the river to Thayaung on the east bank and carry out a short propaganda march in the direction of Japanese post at Thetla in the hope that I might succeed in irritating them a little.

In the middle of October therefore with the tracks still deep in mud I set off with Sanschak and twelve Gurkhas on a second visit to Minya. We followed the route that I had followed before and spent the night with Tibbetts' platoon who were camped in the Sanpat Chaung. He himself was expected to arrive in the course of the next few days.

In the morning we moved on to Minya where I was greeted with the bewildering spectacle of some fifty young Shans dressed in Japanese uniforms and carrying enemy weapons drawn up for my inspection along the river front. Realising that a certain amount of ceremonial was expected of me, I walked down the ranks giving as good an imitation as I could manage of an inspecting general and pausing at intervals to exchange a few words with individual levies. Out of the corner of my eye I could see that my own Assam Riflemen were looking completely bewildered by developments. To them the episode seemed too much of a burlesque of the sacred military ritual to be really funny.

After the inspection I was led off once again to the house of the headman of Minya-North End where a sumptuous meal was spread out before me. The village headmen were themselves then very much in the background, and the most influential figure appeared to be a wizened little Burmese called Kya-aung who was organising guerillas for the American officer at Nawngpuawng. Before the war he had been a business contractor in Tamanthi in the north which had been river head for the Chindwin steamer service and he was obviously in Greek's guerillas for what he could make out of them. The Americans were probably paying him two or three times what he could have hoped to receive from the British, and in addition with them the pickings were probably greater. Nevertheless I found myself rather liking Kya-aung. He was evidently an efficient organiser of levies and he seemed to have instilled the fear of God into the inhabitants of Minya. Doubtless these last were under his regime being somewhat exploited, but in view of their past record I felt very little sympathy for them.

I told him that I wished to cross the Chindwin the following day and intended patrolling as far as either Paungbyin to the south or Tawmagon, a village a few miles inland to the east. Kya-aung said that he would make the necessary arrangements. The Gurkhas and I spent the night in the house of the Minya headman who looked a nervous and much chastened man. He explained to me at great length what precautions he had taken for the defence of the village. In the middle of the room there was a great brass bell hanging from the ceiling, and he told me that if this was struck the whole village would spring to arms ready to repel an enemy attack and if necessary to die to the last man in the process.

As I settled in a corner of the room with my blanket around my shoulders and my groundsheet beneath me, I felt very nearly as bewildered as the Gurkhas. Kya-aung's organisation was evidently most efficient in certain ways, but I felt that the Civil Affairs Service would not approve of it. I however was not a civilian, and Kya-aung had entertained my men and me and was going forth into an enemy sphere of influence with us the following day. I decided that for what it was worth, Kya-aung should have my support when the inevitable clash came between him and the

Burma Government representatives in the Kabaw Valley.

The following day was more like a sporting progress than a warlike operation. After an early meal my party crossed the Chindwin to Thayaung in a fleet of country boats. As we approached the far bank I could see a force of over a hundred levies wearing Japanese uniforms drawn up in the village. For a few moments I felt slightly uneasy, wondering whether I might not be walking into an elaborately laid trap. Then I decided that everything was far too elaborate for treachery.

Thayaung was a large village with a fine stretch of cultivated paddy land stretching out to the east behind it. In peacetime the principal rice merchants had been a family of Sikhs who owned an imposing looking two-storied teak building standing on stilts beside the waterfront. It was there that I adjourned with the reception committee after I had inspected the levies.

Bananas and Shan tea were served while Kya-aung discussed my plans for the day rather in the manner of a gamekeeper advising on where the best sport was to be obtained. The Japanese were in position south of Paungbyin in some strength and were patrolling up to the town itself daily. The place had been badly damaged by bombing and no one was living there, and was of little interest to me. On the other hand Tawmagon to the east was an important rice centre where Kya-aung was already enlisting a section of levies, and it might be of some value to the cause if an Allied officer were to show himself in the place. Kya-aung was evidently very anxious that I should visit Tawmagon and I saw no reason why I should not humour him, so we set off in an easterly direction after we had finished our tea.

On the outskirts of the village I ran into a very old Sikh with a long white beard. Having once served in a Punjabi regiment I paused a moment to pass the time of day with him. He was the owner of the house in which I had drunk tea at Thayaung. As a young man he had served in the Army in Burma, and had settled there after taking his discharge. He had virtually retired before the war, and it was his eldest son who had been running the business in Thayaung. He told me that the last few years since the coming of the Japanese had been very difficult. As an Indian in Burma, he was glad to see the British back.

The track to Tawmagon was in that season deep in mud. For many miles it ran across fields that were still covered by water. In front of my party moved a screen of Shan scouts. Kya-aung seemed most concerned about my comfort and whenever we came to a stream suggested that his men should carry me across. But I resolutely refused these offers.

We moved across a fairytale countryside of bright unspoilt Shan villages clustering around fine pagodas set amidst clumps of trees in a rich rice plain. There was little evidence of the ravages of war. At Tawmagon we drank tea in the headman's house and Kya-aung produced a battered old exercise book from the little coloured cloth bag that he carried over one shoulder and started inscribing in it a long list of names. Since my arrival in Shan country I had noticed that the standard of literacy was higher there than in India. It was fashionable in the Army at that time to regard all Buddhist priests as a parasite element in the community, but they certainly fulfilled a most useful purpose as educationalists.

When the time came to set forth on the return journey I found a fleet of carts drawn by water buffaloes had been marshalled in readiness for myself and the Gurkhas. These had been arranged for by Kya-aung while we had been drinking our tea in the village.

Feeling that this was a fitting climax to what had been a slightly absurd day's travel, I clambered into the leading cart with Kya-aung and the Gurkha Havildar and settled down for the slow rather uncomfortable journey back to Thayaung. This took much longer than the journey out. The carts were at times submerged up to their axles in deep liquid mud and the water buffaloes had to be driven unmercifully. Darkness fell while we were still on the way. By that time my force was straggling badly over a wide area, and I felt that I should have been severely called to task if any one in authority could have seen it. Kya-aung was waxing talkative on his side of the cart. He kept on telling me that the Japanese were very bad people. Then he would draw his finger across his throat at the same time rolling his eyes in a terrifying piece of pantomime and murmuring savagely in Burmese: 'English, Gurkhas. All prisoners killed.' I was rather glad when we arrived safely in Thayaung.

In the village there was a big gathering of Shan levies dressed and armed with captured Japanese equipment. A sumptuous feast

of rice and chicken and many varieties of vegetable had been laid out in the old Sikh's house which was lit for the occasion with hurricane lanterns. The old gentleman had not been able to attend himself but he had sent his son, a pleasant young fellow of about thirty, to do the honours of the house in his absence. My meal was laid on a little table with a single chair beside it on a raised dais. Below in the body of the room the Gurkhas were arranged along both sides of a long refectory table which was also laden with good food. It was rather like a school tea after a football match with me in the role of the housemaster at the high table. Kya-aung and the Shan *lugyis* ate their meal more democratically squatting on the floor. Outside the levies moved back and forwards in the darkness. After the meat course there was fruit and some excellent Burmese cheroots. Everyone seemed to be enjoying themselves immensely.

After it was over I was led upstairs to a bedroom on the first floor where in addition to the old Army blanket that I carried in my pack a fine coloured quilt and mattress had been spread out on the floor. After Kya-aung had gone I felt a little guilty at the very unmilitary manner in which I had visited Tawmagon. Then I decided that perhaps in this case by our very nonchalance we had shown how completely we despised the enemy and in this way impressed Kya-aung and his levies more than if we had taken all orthodox military precautions. At any rate I had enjoyed myself hugely and eaten the best meal since I had arrived on the Burma front nearly two years before.

Back in my own camp at Thaungdut I wrote out a long report to Colonel Stanley on developments at Minya, in which I urged that Kya-aung and his levies were essentially a pro-Allied guerilla organisation, and not, as it was being suggested, a band of dacoits. In this I was born out by his behaviour a few days later when the Assam Regiment company commander sent a strong fighting patrol about a platoon strong down to Paungbyin. Kya-aung moved down in support of this force with about fifty armed levies. South-east of Paungbyin they came upon an enemy post strongly entrenched beneath the houses of a village and there was a brisk little battle in which several men were killed and wounded on both sides. Kya-aung's levies lost two dead. But the representatives of the Burma Civil Affairs Service had already been infuriated by Kya-aung when they heard that he was referring to himself as the Sub-Divisional Officer of Minya, a post in the hierarchy of civilian government, and shortly afterwards he was arrested and removed to Tamu. At the same time Greek, the American OSS officer at Nawngpuawng, received orders to withdraw his levies north. Tibbetts had in the meantime arrived in Sanpat and two other V Force officers, called Speirs and Lindsay, had moved into position on my left flank at Homalin.

My sub-area had reverted to comparative unimportance. There was a company of the Assam Regiment close by, and on the opposite side of the Chindwin no news of the enemy. It was sometime before I met Tibbetts, my closest neighbour. He was a very practically minded young metallurgist from the Midlands with a sound leavening of common sense that gave him the solution to most problems that he came up against. He had been in the siege of Kohima and was badly in need of leave, but in spite of this and recurrent bouts of dysentery he tackled Minya with gusto.

I was surprised one evening when the wizened little headman together with the *thugyis* of its northern and southern suburbs were brought into my camp under arrest by an escort of Tibbetts' Gurkhas en route for Myothit. Unfortunately the Civil refused to back Tibbetts up, although he had the clearest evidence that they had been in communication with the renegade Buddhist priest called U-Nandiya, who was running an enemy spy organisation from Paungbyin on the east bank of the river, and the three recalcitrants were released a few days later.

Relations between V Force and the Civil were becoming somewhat strained. They had recently discovered that we were in possession of an elephant train and had at once deprived us of it. Next they objected to our employing the local villagers as coolies except through their offices. As they were back in Tamu and we were on the Chindwin this was in practice an unsatisfactory arrangement. Doubtless it was essential that they should justify their existence at headquarters, but it was extremely irritating that they should do it at the expense of such hard pressed people as ourselves.

There was in the area a wicked old Shan called Lanbya who had in the very early days of the war been condemned to death as a spy and escaped. His most recent exploit had been to hand over an RAF pilot, who had had to bale out in the Kabaw Valley, to the Japanese during the occupation. To the ordinary fighting soldier it seemed justice that he should be condemned to death for such a crime but the Civil Government conceived the idea that he should be released and sent into the Thaungdut-Minya area to try and induce U-Nandiya and other pro-Japanese Burmese to come over to the British lines and surrender. This plan was put into effect, and Tibbetts, the Assam Regiment and I were all instructed not to arrest him if he should pass our way. I passed these instructions on to my agents and then forgot about the matter.

I had decided to make personal contact with the Americans across the river, as I did not wish them to feel that it was as a result of representations made by me that Kya-aung had been arrested. Accordingly I crossed the river one morning with Sanschak and fourteen Gurkhas at Dokthida and then moved north east through open teak forest to a cultivated area called Myene about four miles inland where we slept the night. The place had evidently been a big Japanese concentration area prior to the Chindwin crossings, and we followed one of their telephone lines inland all the way.

The following day we moved on into the forest in the same direction and, at nightfall, came out into a cultivated paddy area running north and south at a village called Tonzi. The place was marked as a gold mine on the map but this must have been abandoned many years before. The villagers were very nervous of us when we arrived. In the jungle beside the track I stumbled on a disused enemy defensive position. It was one of a chain of similar positions built by the Japanese after the first Chindit operation. The villagers told me that when the Japanese had arrived they had shot the headman and most of the village *lugyis* as a reprisal for their having helped some of Wingate's men in their escape.

East of the Tonzi valley there was another belt of the monotonous open teak jungle which we entered the following morning. Sanschak and the Gurkhas were all reluctant to go any further east, but I felt that the patrol would have lacked any value if we did not move into country where we might obtain first hand information about the enemy, and I insisted on going on. At about two o'clock in the afternoon we came out of the jungle into a cultivated area at a village called Tatkon where there was another very large abandoned Japanese defensive position centred around what must have been a very nearly impregnable bunker. To the north the path ran in the direction of Greek's headquarters at Nawngpuawng about nine miles distant, and to the south lay Sinlamaung about the same distance away.

The headman, who was a tall gaunt-looking Shan with a young and pretty wife and many children, seemed friendly. He told me that the enemy had re-crossed to the western side of the Zibyutaungdan and had re-occupied Sinlamaung. When I asked him how many Americans there were in Nawngpuawng, he told me there were several hundred.

After we had made tea, I set off up the valley to the north along what must have been a dry weather motor road built by the Japs. Just outside the village I walked straight into a tall good-looking young V Force officer with some Assam Riflemen, who turned out to be Lindsay from Homalin. He had left Greek's headquarters that morning and was on his way back to his own camp. The latest reports from the chain of American guerilla units that connected the Chindwin with General Stilwell's Chinese on the Irrawaddy was that the Japanese in the gap between the two armies had shown considerable activity during the last few days and had driven the levies north in several places. Greek and Lindsay had been in position in a village well to the south of Tatkon just north of Sinlamaung, where they had been very nearly surrounded by the enemy, and obliged to flee north to Nawngpuawng. Some of Greek's Kachins had been captured. The report that there were several hundred Americans at Nawngpuawng was a false one that Greek was doing his best to circulate for his own protection. In fact there were only three. The previous night Greek and Lindsay had made a quick night march south to an abandoned enemy ammunition dump east of Tatkon which they had blown up.

Saying good-bye to Lindsay I moved on up the valley through several large Shan villages set in the midst of clumps of trees and surrounded on all sides by fields of growing rice. At nightfall we were some four miles south of Nawngpuawng, and I decided to call a halt. I felt that the Americans might have ambush parties out in front of their position which might mistake us for Japanese in the darkness.

There seemed no shortage of food in the village and we were given a rice meal. I was rather surprised when the Buddhist priest in his orange robe came in to see me. Usually the *hpongyis* held themselves aloof, but this one seemed prepared to be friendly. He spoke Kachin and was disappointed that I was unable to do likewise. In appearance the Gurkhas are not unlike the Kachins in the north of Burma and at first sight he had probably believed that my men were of that race.

The next morning we moved on to Nawngpuawng. Approaching the village from the south we passed across a large open space which had been laid out as a landing strip for aeroplanes where a party of levies were drilling under some Burmese NCOs wearing American uniforms. Beyond it an untidy village street straggled for about two hundred yards to the bank of the Uyu River. The place must have been a wealthy centre of civilisation in the old days, for there were a number of large buildings collected along the river bank. Greek himself was shaving on the verandah of the *dak* bungalow.

He was a most amusing and forceful personality whose real name was Kasouli. Like all the OSS officers in North Burma, however, he went under a nickname for security reasons. He was stocky and thick set with jet black hair and a sophisticated little moustache. He was the excitable, talkative type of American, and was, as his pseudonym implied, of Greek origin. The day I arrived, he was in fine form after his destruction of the enemy ammunition dump with Lindsay.

During the course of the morning several L5 pilots landed on the strip and came over for a cup of coffee to Greek's headquarters. For the benefit of each of them Greek went through a magnificent routine of stretching voluptuously and slapping his very muscular thighs. This was but a prelude to the story of the ammunition dump episode which he would preface with the words: 'Gee, I feel just the way I used to feel after a tough football game back in the States.' He had originally been recruited into the OSS for service in Greece, but the operations had in some way or other failed to take place and he had been posted east.

He broke nearly all the rules that a British-style levy officer would have considered it vital to obey, and yet he was a popular figure among the Shans. To give just a single example: the Shans, like most orientals, are sensitive about bathing in the nude in public, and most westerners made their ablutions in a pair of underpants in order not to offend these local sensibilities. But daily Greek would appear on the verandah of the *dak* bungalow in all his naked splendour in full view of the entire village. He was a powerful enough personality to be able to flout conventions and his eccentricities were tacitly accepted.

It was arranged that I should spend the day with Greek and continue my journey the next morning. It was a most amusing experience to live for a few hours in this little outpost of Americanism in its exotic setting. Greek had two sergeant operators, who were equally typical of a different variety of American. They were tall fair-haired slow-spoken young men of Polish and German origin respectively.

During the afternoon a Dakota landed on the airfield and about thirty visitors from Imphal descended on the *dak* bungalow for coffee. I was at the time wearing an American uniform lent me by Greek until such time as my own tunic and slacks should have been properly dried. But everyone recognised me as a Britisher on account of the redness of my face. Among them was a tall shy young English major whose hair was thinning prematurely at the temples called George Scurfield. He had just been appointed as second-in-command to Colonel Stanley in 2 V Ops and had been sent over with an American liaison officer to tie up the contacts between the two irregular formations.

During the course of the coffee party a tall slow-spoken Texan who had arrived on the plane and who had been studying Greek without comment for some time leant forward in his chair and said in a lazy drawl: 'You remind me of a full-back I used to play football against back in the States called Kasouli.' There was an electric silence. Greek grinned delightedly and thumped his chest. 'I *am* Kasouli,' he said proudly.

That night Greek was still in splendid form and told us at great

length of his earlier adventures in the Army. He was a delightfully
frank person. In civilian life he had been a cinema proprietor in
Altoona, Pennsylvania. When the war had broken out he had filled
in an application form for a post in the United States' equivalent
of ENSA, but they had called him up as an infantryman before he
had been able to send it in. On his arrival at the infantry camp
when they discovered his Greek origin the top sergeant had at
once set him to work in the cook-house as a potato peeler
extraordinary. But eventually his merits had been recognised and
he had been commissioned.

I enjoyed my stay with the Americans and was grateful to them
for their quite overwhelming hospitality. The next day I returned
to Thaungdut by boat.

I did not see Greek again until two months later just before the
Irrawaddy crossing at Thabekyin. When I got back to my
headquarters above Thaungdut it had already ceased to be a
guerilla area in the true sense of the word. The company of the
Assam Regiment had been relieved by a larger detachment from a
battalion of the Bombay Grenadiers, and it had apparently been
decided that the 19th Indian Division would cross the Chindwin at
Tonnhe in the middle of November and advance on Mandalay on
the left flank of the main drive that was to pass through Kalewa
well to the south.

During the last weeks of October and the first fortnight of
November the monsoon drew to a close and relays of sappers and
miners assisted by Shan coolies laboured to make the track across
the mountains from Thanan in the Kabaw valley into a motor
road. I made myself as useful as possible to the regular troops as
an organiser of guides and coolies.

To the south of me Tibbetts was having a more interesting time.
A Japanese salvage party had recrossed the Zibyutaungdan and
moved back along the old motor road removing the engines from
their abandoned vehicles and clearing what they could of the store
dumps that had been left on the east bank of the river. Tibbetts
and an Anglo-American intelligence unit that concerned itself with
the study of captured enemy equipment crossed one night under
the noses of the enemy and blew up twelve medium guns in the

Teak forest north of the Thayaung rice plain.

Then one day a very wicked looking old Shan arrived at my camp under an escort of Tibbetts' men, protesting loudly. He was being taken to Colonel Stanley's camp at Myothit and I saw from the accompanying letter that he had been guilty of handing a British pilot over to the enemy during the occupation. The old reprobate told me his name was Lanbya and although it sounded vaguely familiar I put it out of my mind. Then while I was eating my supper the same night I remembered the Civil Affairs Service's much heralded secret agent who was under no circumstances to be interfered with. His name had been Lanbya too. Hurrying over to the hut in which he was imprisoned, I soon discovered that this fellow and the secret agent were one and the same person. Very reluctantly I released him, and during the next few days expected a severe reprimand from higher up. But Lanbya had probably far too guilty a conscience to complain of his night's imprisonment at Tibbetts' and my hands, and we heard nothing more of the matter.

When the time came the 19th Divisions's crossing of the Chindwin was unopposed. They were a magnificent body of men who were if anything slightly overtrained, and they were thirsting for battle. I believe that they were genuinely disappointed when the Japanese salvage parties along the motor road withdrew before them without firing a shot. The plan for 2 V Ops had been that it should provide an intelligence screen on 19 Division's left flank. But with their jeeps and motor transport they advanced so rapidly across the Zibyutaungdan that on our flat feet we were barely able to keep up with them.

On the other side of the hills we came again into another rice plain where 19 Division turned south in the direction of Shwebo. Behind them 2 V Ops and the American guerilla units, who being also without any transport, were in the same predicament, were striving desperately by a series of forced marches to keep up with the regular troops. Nowhere did the enemy appear to be making a stand.

As December opened the cold season came upon us. This is a very beautiful and attractive time in Burma. At night the temperature falls to a little above freezing point, but by day the sun shines as brightly as it does at the height of an English

Elephant transport in Karenni

Hyena Area Headquarters Staff on Mount Plakho

summer. Day after day we marched on down the long dusty road to Mandalay through a strange secret world of empty villages and ruined pagodas.

North of Pinlebu Colonel Stanley, who was worried about the fact that our unit was no longer playing a very vital role in the war, had one of those strokes of almost intuitive genius that made him into a great irregular leader. Judging that sooner or later Japanese resistance would stiffen before the regular troops arrived at the junction of the Chindwin and Irrawaddy Rivers and that in any case 19 Division would inevitably get orders to jink left when it finally came onto the same axis of advance as the British 2nd Division, he sent Gillett and me across to the Irrawaddy to collect a fleet of country boats and bamboo rafts with which we could later help the regular troops to cross the river.

I spent a week at a little Burmese village called Tigyaing, holding conference with headmen and supervising the construction of two enormous rafts of bamboo on which we estimated that a 15-cwt lorry could be ferried across the river. Meanwhile Gillett crossed to the opposite bank where a brigade of the British 36th Division under the command of the American Northern Combat Area was advancing slowly against light opposition down the east bank.

When the rafts were ready and we had assembled twelve very large country boats into the bargain we set off along the east bank with an American Kachin guerilla unit. For two days we drifted gently downstream keeping contact with a battalion of the Royal Scots Fusiliers on the east bank. At Kyannyat these were held up and the Americans received orders to cross behind them. At the same time we received a message from Colonel Stanley that he had himself reached the Irrawaddy at a point to the south. Accordingly we waited till after darkness and then put out into midstream and drifted past the enemy positions under cover of the night. At dawn we reached Male where Stanley had set up his headquarters.

All the officers of 2 V Ops were sleeping on the floor of a ruined pagoda underneath the image of the Buddha. They had decided that they would be better spending their time on leave in India, and I think that we did not make matters very easy for Colonel Stanley. But he persevered in pushing patrols across the

Irrawaddy which brought in some useful information and the
indomitable Gillett captured a prisoner.

In the meantime the situation had developed very much as
Colonel Stanley had anticipated. Two Division and 19 Division
had effected a junction at Shwebo and the latter had been ordered
to move east across the Irrawaddy in the direction of Mogok.
Information from Thabekyin, the northernmost point at which it
was intended to cross the river, was to the effect that there were
no boats available and V Force had been asked to help. I was
ordered to move south with my twelve country boats to
Thabekyin. Nineteen Division were not apparently interested in
the rafts, which were considered difficult to navigate.

The night before I left we received orders from Imphal that
2 V Ops was to withdraw to India for reorganisation and further
training. All officers were to proceed on leave. This was the signal
for great jubilation. It was arranged that Tibbetts and I should be
the first to go. He was to march east the following day to a nearby
landing strip, and I was to proceed to another at Onbauk close to
Shwebo as soon as I had handed over the boats to 19 Division at
Thabekyin.

I left at dawn and spent the morning drifting placidly
downstream. Towards midday as we approached Thabekyin I
heard automatic fire in the distance and I ordered the men to
disembark on the right bank. We drew up the boats into a small
subsidiary *chaung*, and I went forward on foot. In the village I
found Greek with a Japanese—American Top Sergeant called Karl
and an Anglo-Burmese interpreter called Jimmie. Greek told me he
was on a special mission and was looking rather glum. Apparently
he and his men were infested with lice and were without rations
and he reckoned they were all going to be killed.

I went on down the bank to contact the Gurkha battalion that
had just arrived from Onbauk. The Colonel very kindly ordered
two of the trucks that had brought his battalion to remain there
overnight and take my party back to Onbauk in the morning.
After that I took a company commander back to the point where
I had left the boats and handed them over to him. Then I went
back to see the Gurkha Quartermaster and beg some rations for

Greek's party. Like most Americans, although he was quite promiscuously generous when he had anything to give away, he was strangely reluctant to ask a favour from anyone else when he was himself in need.

We ate a melancholy meal of rice and bully beef. Greek had had orders to make a personal reconnaissance on the opposite back of the river as far as Mogok, which was, as far as we knew, an area in which large numbers of Japanese troops were then concentrated. Jimmie suggested that they should stay where they were and invent some good reports to send back over the wirelesss. He reckoned that as long as they reported that there were many Japs in the Mogok area they were certain to be correct. But Greek decided that such a course of conduct would be dishonest, and that one or the other of them would have to go to Mogok and get himself killed.

Having come to this dismal conclusion he cheered up considerably and held us all spellbound throughout the rest of the evening with an account of life in Altoona, Pennsylvania. In the morning both sides started shooting at each other across the river and Greek was ordered to go back to India.

I set off for Onbauk with my Gurkhas in the two trucks. There were reports of odd Japanese jitter parties on the road, but we passed through without meeting a soul. At about eleven o'clock, however, the Jemedar, who was sitting beside me drew my attention to seventeen fighter aircraft flying above us. They looked like Spitfires, but their wings reflected the sun, I assured him comfortably that to my certain knowledge they were our own planes, and just after I had done so they dived onto the road about a mile ahead of us and we could hear their guns going. After that we proceeded very much more carefully, and reached the airfield at Onbauk without further event.

There there appeared to be great chaos. It had been raided in the morning by the seventeen Zeros that we had seen, and two Dakotas had been destroyed on the ground. I was told that it was unlikely that any further aeroplanes would come in from Imphal that day. We spent a very miserable three hours sitting in the sun beside the supply dump, and then the sound of an aeroplane engine came to our ears. Everyone dived into their slit trenches, but it turned out to be another Dakota, which took my party back to Imphal.

Two days later I was flown out to Calcutta on leave with Tibbetts.

PART THREE

Karenni

1

In Calcutta Tibbetts and I fell in with two other V Force officers called Bill Scott and Roger Whitaker at Spenser's Hotel, a rather interesting old world establishment run by a very well-known Calcutta figure of over seventy called Harry Hobbs, who contributed a daily anecdote to *Seac*, the soldiers' newspaper in South East Asia Command. This hotel became a great rendezvous for V Force personnel and as the rest of them were evacuated from the Irrawaddy our numbers grew. Calcutta was at that time full to overflowing with British and American troops all very anxious to enjoy a hectic leave. Prices had reached inflationary levels and I found myself living at the rate of £4 per day without in any way indulging in blatant extravagances. Fortunately after two years in the operational area without a break I was by way of being temporarily a very wealthy young man.

Since the days when I had been in the Punjabi battalion I had always intended to make a pilgrimage to the cradle of the regiment. My companions were indifferent as to where they spent their leave and agreed that we should go to Lahore in the Punjab as soon as we could get a reservation on one of the trains. But in the meantime Roger Whitaker became enamoured of an attractive young FANY and when Scott and he learned that we should have to spend four days in the train on the journey to the north they talked Tibbetts and me into going to Darjeeling instead.

In Darjeeling there was snow on the ground and very few people in the hotels. Roger and Scott were from the start discontented with the place and returned to Calcutta after a few days, but Tibbetts and I settled ourselves into a very comfortable room at the Mount Everest Hotel and spent a healthy fortnight riding, reading, sleeping and eating interspersed with some convivial evenings in the local bars. Both of us were at that time rather sick men and the cold mountain air did a great deal to restore our health.

In the meantime the Groups of V Force that had formerly been centred on Imphal and Lushai were reforming in a camp at Shillong, a pleasant hill station in Assam about 7,000 feet above sea level. When Tibbetts and I rejoined after our leave, we found ourselves committed to a mixed programme of wireless training and lectures on the organisation of the Japanese army.

The possibility of V Force ever fulfilling its original role as a post-occupation guerilla force had faded into the background, but it had been decided not to disband it. Instead it was to be mechanised and re-equipped with some light portable wireless sets and used for intelligence purposes wherever Fourteenth Army might see fit to send it. A Group, which had formerly been known as Assam Zone to which 2 and 3 V Ops belonged, was then under command of a young South African mining engineer called Jerry Hayter. Jerry was a stockily built young man of thirty-one, who was delightfully informal in his relations with his junior officers. He was never happy when we addressed him as 'Sir'. I always made a point of doing so whenever a third person was present and he always looked slightly embarrassed. V Force was a difficult command in that practically no one in it had any administrative ability whatsoever, but somehow or other Jerry contrived to keep it functioning efficiently.

Pip Fraser-Smith had been given command of 3 V Ops and as I had originally been a member of that unit before my sub-area had been transferred to Stanley on the Chindwin, it was arranged that I should be posted back to them together with George Scurfield. Then Pip Fraser-Smith had a bad accident during a game of soccer with the Gurkhas and was sent off to England on leave. In his absence George Scurfield took command of 3 V Ops and I was promoted major as his second in command.

George was an interesting personality. Before the war he had been an undergraduate at St John's College, Cambridge, where he had been reading English, and he gave the appearance of being many years older than he really was. He liked to create the impression that he was of a nervous disposition, but he had been awarded the MC and been mentioned in despatches and was perhaps in a better position than most people to admit his fears without being taken very seriously.

At that time 3 V Ops was somewhat under strength. In addition, to myself, there were only four other officers. Three of these, David Bridges, Jim Murray and Jock Longmuir, were Scots, and the fourth, Joe Bennett, was a quiet little bespectacled Englishman who had spent most of the war arguing his way out of a heavy anti-aircraft unit into something more adventurous. David and Jim were both very typical Lowlanders with a very wide range of interests and a careful attitude towards life. Jock was a wild generous Highlander from Nairn with tremendous courage, who was killed just at the time of the Japanese surrender. He had a little daughter in Scotland of whom he was very proud.

Soon after our arrival in Shillong we were asked whether we were prepared to train as parachutists. Every officer in A Group volunteered, and as I had only the previous week been promoted major I felt that I could not in all decency refrain. 2 V Ops was the first unit in Shillong to be brought up to strength and issued with the requisite number of vehicles. Early in April 1945 they were ordered to move off to Burma by road. Jerry and his small headquarters staff went with them. 3 V Ops was left in a disappointed and disgruntled mood. The monsoon was due to break in June and from that time the roads into Burma would be closed until the following December at least and it seemed unlikely that we should be able to move before the end of the year. All the officers in 3 V Ops were due for repatriation within the next few months, and we were afraid that we should be expected to defer this until after we had done another operation. And then Jerry sent a wild and mysterious signal from Fourteenth Army headquarters at Monywa in Central Burma to the effect that he was coming back to Shillong with special orders for 3 V Ops and that all Gurkha and other personnel who had volunteered to parachute should be kitted up in readiness to move.

After the fall of Mandalay early in 1945 there had been very fierce Japanese resistance on the motor road which led to Rangoon. Then the 4th Indian Corps made a surprise thrust across the Irrawaddy to the south on the enemy's lines of communication, capturing the airfield at Meiktila, and the Japanese forces that had been opposing the 19th Indian Division to the north had been obliged to withdraw east into the foothills of the Shan States. When our armoured thrust developed along the motor road running south from Meiktila through Pyinmana, Toungoo and Pegu to Rangoon the Japanese had not enough heavy equipment left in Burma to oppose it, and their troops escaped either westwards into the dense jungle-covered foothills known as the Pegu Yomas, where they linked up with their comrades from Prome and the Arakan or eastwards across the Sittang River.

On the east of the Sittang there is flat paddy country for a distance of ten to fifteen miles and then the ground rises very steeply into the Karen Hills, which run as high as seven thousand feet in a few places and stretch beyond the Salween River into Siam. These hills grow enough rice to feed the Karen villagers who live in them. Before the war there was a tin mine at Mawchi which was worked by Gurkha miners. Except for this there was really no reason for strangers ever to penetrate into that country and the people led a healthy happy life with plenty to eat and very little to trouble them. Some of the more adventurous Karens had penetrated into the Burmese plains at an earlier date, and in the way that hardy mountain people do had proved more than a match for the easygoing Burmese plainsmen. This penetration into Burma proper had not endeared them to the Burmese, and they would doubtless have been persecuted as a too energetic minority if the British administration had not been there to protect their interests.

When the Japanese invaded Burma in 1942, the Burmese had on the whole been sympathetic towards them but the loyalty of the Karens to the British had never for a moment wavered. While the Burma Army was retreating slowly north up the Toungoo road a Burma Rifles officer called Major Seagrim was sent off into the Karen hills to raise levies and watch the crossing places on the Salween until such time as the regular troops had escaped to the north of Toungoo. He carried out this task successfully, but at the close of it was unable to rejoin the main British force. Opinion varies as to whether he could really have done so if he had wanted to, but the fact remains that he was left behind.

To begin with the Japanese were probably unaware of Seagrim's presence in the hills. He lived in a bamboo hut in the jungle near an obscure little mountain village called Pyagawpu, where the people are all Karens and no one was likely to carry information to the *Kempei Tai* at Papun or in the Sittang Valley. But eventually rumours to the effect that a mysterious Britisher was living in the mountains must have found their way down to cosmopolitan bazaar areas like Kyaukkyi where Karens rubbed shoulders with Shans and Burmans and in the end the matter came to Japanese ears.

About this time also the British Government received word through its agents in the Burma Delta that Seagrim was still alive, and shortly afterwards a young Karen called Saw Thet Wa who had fled to India at the time of the Japanese invasion and later enlisted in the RAF was trained as a wireless operator and put into Karenni by parachute.

Saw Thet Wa found Seagrim very easily and a wireless link with India was established. The Karens from as far north as Mawchi and as far south as Papun were aware of Seagrim's existence and contacts had even been made with Karen communities living in the Delta and at Moulmein. But at this stage it was too early to organise an offensive resistance movement and Seagrim's policy was to instruct all his followers to co-operate with the Japanese to the best of their abilities and to keep him informed of all that was going on.

It must have been a source of considerable embarrassment to him when one of his henchmen, a former Naik in the Burma Rifles who had become separated from his unit in the original retreat and had taken to the hills, seized some Government offices south of Papun where the Japanese puppet adminstration was established and hoisted the Union Jack. The revolt, if it can be referred to by such a grandiloquent title, was soon suppressed and the unfortunate Naik executed.

At this time two more British officers, Nimmo and McCrindle, were put into Karenni by parachute, and the Japanese started to send bodies of troops and security police into the hills in a concentrated drive against the guerillas. Prior to this no action had been taken against Seagrim, probably because he was not regarded as a potential source of revolt, but only as a survivor of the original Burma retreat. But now the *Kempei Tai* started to operate in the hills with great ferocity, torturing all suspects until they related what they knew of Seagrim's whereabouts, and the guerillas were kept continually on the move.

Both Nimmo and McCrindle were captured and executed. But Seagrim always escaped his pursuers, although by this time he was a very sick man without boots or any European clothing. Finally he came to the conclusion that by his presence in Karenni he was the direct cause of the tribesmen being oppressed, and he surrendered to the Japanese. In a very dramatic trial he asked his judges not to punish the Karens for what he had persuaded them to do and to hold him personally fully responsible. He was executed and the last British contact in Karenni went dead until February 1945 when a party of parachutists under Major Turrall dropped into Pyagawpu.

Turrall was a short wiry little prospector from Rhodesia aged fifty-three, who had been awarded and MC in the First World War, and afterwards served with Wingate's Gideon Force in Abyssinia. He had come to Burma in the first instance to run a deception unit in the second Chindit operation where his task had been to lay the trails, noises and effects of a Chindit Brigade that did not in fact exist. His reception in Pyagawpu must have been somewhat mixed, for the Karens cannot have been very well informed as to the course of the war, and the regular troops were indeed at that time no nearer than Mandalay. But when a further party of Britishers arrived the following night the locals began to gain confidence. The night Turrall had jumped there had actually been a Burmese policeman from the Japanese puppet police force quartered in the local police station. The headman and village elders had suggested that this worthy might be quietly dispatched, but Turrall refused to countenance an act which he thought might lead to reprisals being taken against the countryside, and the man was allowed to escape in the direction of Papun.

At the time of the arrival of the second party of parachutists at Pygawpu a British captain called Duncan Guthrie and a Shan irregular parachutist had both broken their ankles. Two days later one of the Sergeant wireless operators called Moore burned his hand very badly with a phosphorous flare when in the process of burning papers. So that when news was received that a party of Japanese was advancing from the direction of Papun a number of problems arose. It was not considered sound to start attacking the Japanese until such time as the regular forces reached the area of Toungoo, and accordingly Guthrie, Moore and the Shan were all hidden in the jungle on a neighbouring mountain called Plakho, and Turrall and the remainder of the party moved off in the direction of Kyaukkyi.

The first Japanese party to approach the area from Papun was a small one consisting of *Kempei Tai*. The story goes that as they approached Pyagawpu they made continual enquiries as to whether any British parachutists were in the area. It was useless for the villagers to deny all knowledge of them, so they adopted the plan of looking particularly vacant and telling the Japanese that they had heard tell that there had been parachutists, but that they had no knowledge of where or in what numbers.

Finally very close to Pyagawpu one old Karen excelled himself. The *Kempei Tai* had been grilling him relentlessly, and he was finally forced to admit that there had been parachutists in Pyagawpu. The Japanese began insisting upon details, and in the end he pointed knowledgeably to a bamboo hut about a quarter of a mile distant across the fields and then with a sweep of his arm intimating the distance that intervened, told the Japanese that from that hut to the spot on which they stood the fields had been thick with parachutists. The Japanese beat a hasty retreat in the direction of Papun, and when they returned the following week they brought a battalion of troops with them.

Guthrie, Moore and the Shan had a hair-raising three weeks on Mount Plakho while the Japanese occupied the police station and searched the area daily. All the villagers had fled east into the wild jungle country around the Yunzalin Chaung, and food was brought to them on the mountain daily by the one armed headman who had remained with them. By the time that the Japanese force withdrew Guthrie's leg had already set and he was no longer suffering great pain, but he was of course a hopeless cripple. In the meantime the regular forces were rapidly approaching Toungoo in their drive on Rangoon, and Turrall had lighted the fires rather earlier than was strictly necessary by occupying the little market town of Kyaukkyi and setting up a People's Committee to defend the place. Turrall had himself been wounded in the attack and obliged to withdraw to the hills immediately afterwards. The success at Kyaukkyi was shortlived, for the Japanese came in at dawn the day after Turrall left, and the Burmese element in the People's Defence Committee surrendered without a fight. But the flag had been shown in Karenni and from that time the war was on.

2

This was the situation that Jerry described when he came back from Army Headquarters. The regular forces had advanced beyond Toungoo in the direction of Rangoon and throughout the Karen hills the tribesmen had risen on the Japanese lines of communication. In the plains where the Burmese predominated another guerilla organisation with more left wing sympathies, known as the Anti-Fascist Organisation, had come into existence, and along with a number of units from the former Burmese Defence Army that had been raised under Japanese auspices, was also joining in the rout of the Japanese forces.

Jerry had offered the services of 3 V Ops in Karenni and these had been accepted by Force 136 who were running the operation. Force 136 was the Far Eastern Section of SOE, and its job was to co-operate with and organise Resistance movements in enemy occupied territory.

Jerry was determined to accompany the operation himself, and planned to leave George Scurfield behind in Shillong to administer what was left of A Group. George decided that his conscience did not allow him to remain in this role and he had a private and probably rather mutinous interview with Jerry late that night. The upshot of it was that Jerry decided that, as I was a married man, I should remain in George's place. I found it impossible not to point out to Jerry that he himself was married, but otherwise held my peace in a fatalistic manner.

The idea of the operation had caught my imagination, and the night before I had decided that I would have just enough courage to do the odd parachute jump necessary to get me into Karenni and that, once there, with the situation deteriorating against the Japanese all the time, everything would be easy. But I could at the same time imagine how my wife would be against my participating, and I decided to leave the whole decision to chance. If Jerry chose to take me, I would go. If he chose not to, my wife at any rate would have been pleased if she had known.

In the morning there was a good deal of excitement in the Gurkha lines with everyone saying good-bye to everyone else and much coming and going and drawing of kit. George felt that it was more to the general interest that Jerry should stay and agitate for our repatriation when it became due and argued with Jerry about it. Most of the other officers intervened on my behalf as well. In the evening the situation took a novel turn when Jerry changed his mind and decided to take me, leaving David Bridges in my place. There was promptly a heated interview between Jerry and David, in which David resigned from V Force, and then it was decided that Ramsbottom, the A Group Intelligence Officer, should be left behind. In the end Ramsbottom also contrived not to remain, but his being detailed to do so put a stop to all argument for that night at any rate.

Early in the war I saw an American film called *Parachute Battalion* which was all about the training of paratroopers. This was before Pearl Harbour, so perhaps a greater emphasis was laid on the dangers of jumping than might have been the case if the directors had been able to rely on a heroic battle climax. At any rate, watching the film one got the impression that a paratrooper's training was very terrifying and rigorous and that one had to be tough to make the grade.

Much to my surprise none of the instructors at the parachute school looked particularly athletic, and I found the fact reassuring. The chief instructor was jovial and plump and went about telling people that there was absolutely nothing in it. As he had himself done more than two hundred and thirty jumps, we were prepared to respect his opinion. Whether I was trained in the way that a British paratrooper normally is, I do not know. But I was certainly eased through my training in a way that was least calculated to frighten me. All the instructors and administrative staff at the school adopted the attitude that any one could do a parachute jump, including girls and old gentlemen, and that one had absolutely nothing to fear.

The first day was to be devoted to ground training, and safe in the knowledge that we would not do a jump until the morrow I besported myself with a squad of Gurkhas under a Sergeant

Instructor. The rolls seemed easy enough and both my men and I gained confidence progressively throughout the day, until just before tea-time. When we expected the parade to be dismissed, the chief instructor let out the bombshell that we were to jump that evening after all. I do not know whether it was purely by chance that we were not told of this change of plan until the last minute. But the arrangement was a happy one, for we had very little time in which to feel afraid.

After drawing our parachutes, we were piled into trucks and taken down to the airfield where two Dakotas were awaiting us with their propellers already turning. The Gurkhas looked like a group of little gnomes in their parachute harness with their shock absorbers on their heads. A very tough old Quartermaster Sergeant, who had been an instructor at the Gurkha Parachute Training Centre at Chaklala and who spoke Gurkhali, had been borrowed for the occasion by the staff when they learned that Gurkhas were going to jump that day. He kept the men laughing by singing a succession of bawdy songs in Gurkhali as his aeroplane approached the place where we were going to jump.

George Scurfield and I were in the second plane to take off. George was to jump first with a stick of five, followed by another stick of Gurkhas. Then I was to follow with the last stick. I caught George's eye as the Dakota approached the dropping zone and wondered whether he was feeling as uncomfortable as I was. I knew at that stage that it was impossible for me to back out, although I felt that I should have liked to do so very much. I decided that I would certainly be killed but there was absolutely no way out.

The aeroplane in front of us had by this time dropped all its bodies, and the despatcher in ours stationed himself near the door with the parachute instructor and gave the order for the first stick to prepare for action. I watched George and the first four Gurkhas line up in front of the door and hand their static lines in turn to the despatcher whose duty it was to hook them onto the line of fasteners opposite the doorway. Then I saw George standing in front of the doorway looking very grim and then he was out. Probably none of the Gurkhas behind him had ever seen a motor car before they joined the Army, let alone an aeroplane, but none of them faltered. They followed George through the doorway with tense set little faces in a steady stream. The spectacle impressed me and I realised even more than ever before just how impossible it would be for me to halt in the doorway and say No.

I watched the second stick go out with ever increasing foreboding and then it was my turn to hand the end of my static line to the despatcher and move into the doorway. There is a tiny light above one's head, and when it is showing red the despatcher gives the order *'Action stations.Number One'* and the Number One of the stick, which in that case was me, stands facing the door with his hands just round the outside and his left foot forward and toe on the edge of the drop. When the light changes to green, the despatcher says *'Go'*, and the Number One kicks forward with his right leg and goes out into space.

Opinions vary as to whether it is better to be Number One or one of the later numbers. As Number One you can see the ground going by beneath you before you jump, but you do at any rate feel less constricted than if you are standing in the middle of the stick. On both occasions that I jumped I was Number One, and I think if I ever had to do so again I should choose the same position. I found on my second jump that it is possible as Number One to avoid seeing the earth beneath while the stick waits to go, by concentrating one's eyes on the red light on the panel above the door. And then when it changes to green shutting them and lunging forward with one's right foot and pushing back with one's hands.

The slipstream seemed to hit me with great force when I went through the doorway, and I think that I was almost horizontal to the earth until my parachute opened. There is nothing very dangerous about parachute jumping nowadays, but it is a most unnatural method of coming to earth. Once my parachute was open I was overcome with relief and relaxed completely forgetting all about the fundamental rules of ground training that it is essential to land with one's feet together.

As I neared the earth the assembled audience started yelling my name and telling me to close my legs. I remembered just in time, decided that I was going to come in backwards, remembered that the instructor had told me that one should get one's body well forward, and then I was sprawling on my back with a laughing crowd around me.

They did not let us do another practice jump before the operation. Ramsbottom and some of the younger members of the party kept on making tentative enquiries about whether they could jump again, but George and I, strongly supported by an elderly Karen Subedar from the Burma Signals, argued that we might sprain our ankles on a second occasion and so have to be left out of the operation altogether. The instructors at the parachute school fortunately agreed with us and we were all left in peace.

Rangoon fell while we were still at the operational centre waiting for a plane, and we all started to wonder whether the affair would be called off. This was in April and it was extremely hot in the flat rice country outside Calcutta. We had all received our monthly Army liquor ration shortly before, so that there was a great deal to drink in the bungalow in which he lived. Then Jerry went off into Calcutta suddenly, and we were all ordered to follow him the next day. It had been decided that we were to go in in three parties. George Scurfield, David Bridges, Jim Murray and Ramsbottom were to go into what was known as the Otter area operating on the Mawchi–Kemapyu road with two parties of fourteen Gurkhas and some Burma Signals wireless operators. Jerry and I were to go into Hyena area at Pyagawpu in the centre of the mountains with another party, while Basil Flack, the A Group Liaison Officer, and Joe Bennett were to go in on their own to another operation east of Moulmein called Antelope.

We spent the next day in Calcutta being briefed and kitted up and were then driven back to the airfield in the evening. While we were on the operation, we were to be given a Poste Restante address in the Calcutta Post Office; and I wrote a long letter to my wife trying to explain that I would really and truly be repatriated in about three months' time, but that in the meanwhile I was going to do just one more operation which would necessitate my going into a very remote area from which it might be very difficult to write letters. I tried to give the impression that this was outpost duty in a place which had to be watched but which the Japanese were unlikely to visit.

The plan was that we should be dropped into our areas shortly after dawn, which is a very good time for parachute jumping as one descends more gently when the air is cool. It was therefore necessary for the Dakotas to take off from the airfield at three o'clock in the morning. In the circumstances it hardly seemed worth while going to bed, and we spent a rather alcoholic evening in the bar of the operational centre. And then when that closed went back to our bungalow across the road and finished off what remained of our monthly liquor rations. Finally a staff officer appeared whose invidious task it was to see us onto the aeroplanes. He was a very nice fellow who had lived in South America before the war and had just the right manner for the occasion.

Down on the airfield I collected the three Burma Signals and five Gurkhas who were to accompany me on the aeroplane, and we were each issued with a little flask of rum to raise our spirits if that should be necessary. The whole party had had a very alcoholic evening, but we all felt stone cold sober at that hour. The pilot asked if there was any particular route I wanted to take to the target, a question which rather surprised me, but which was, I suppose, intended to have a reassuring effect. I told him I left it all to him.

After the Dakota took off, the Gurkhas and Burma Signals went to sleep on the floor of the aeroplane in the most nonchalant fashion, and I pretended to do likewise. But in spite of all the rum that I had drunk in the course of the evening I could not sleep a wink. About five o'clock it started to get light and I gave up all pretence of sleep and settled down to study the country beneath. We were passing over the Irrawaddy and the jungle looked very remote and mysterious in the early morning mist.

About half an hour later we came into a bank of low cloud, and the despatcher announced that we should probably never be able to find the target. For a moment my hopes rose wildly and I wanted to pray that this might happen. Then I began to picture to myself how very unpleasant it would be to retrace one's steps and try again another day, and in the end I decided that perhaps after all it would be just as well to get everything over once and for all.

I went along to the cabin in the front of the aeroplane and drank a cup of tea with the navigator and wireless operator. I remember thinking what lucky devils they were to be up there in that nice cosy little cabin while I, in a very few minutes, would be going out into space and down into that sinister green countryside beneath. Then I thought that after all I should in an hour's time have my feet on the earth and that afterwards my feet would remain on the earth for ever and ever, but that these poor fellows were doomed to continue on these dreadful journeys through the clouds over dark green countrysides. And I pitied them more than I pitied myself. My thoughts might well have made up the subject for an interesting inter-service argument, but I did not consider that the moment was suitable.

I went back to the Gurkhas in the main body of the Dakota and then the despatcher came back and told us to get dressed. There was still a good deal of cloud about, but the navigator reckoned that we were somewhere near the target. I was fitted into my parachute harness and my maps, shaving materials and one or two other odds and ends were tied around my neck in a little blue bag. I must have appeared an ungainly figure waddling around the fuselage. I settled myself in a corner while the Gurkhas went through the same process and again decided that I was about to be killed, but that there was absolutely no way out at that stage. I admired the *sangfroid* of the Gurkhas who seemed totally unconcerned at what was going on around them. Then the despatcher gave a whoop of delight and I knew that we had found the target. We had come down out of the cloud into a low valley in which a flat long paddy field broken by a network of tiny *bands* or dykes ran between dark green jungle clad hills.

The despatcher beckoned me to come forward along the plane. He hooked up my static line and I went over and stood in the doorway and concentrated on the red light so that I should not see the ground that was going by beneath me. Then it changed to green and I exchanged a grin with the despatcher that in my case must have looked rather sickly. I shut my eyes, drove forward with my chest and right leg at the same time pressing back with my hands. For a moment I was in space, and then there was a tugging at my shoulders and I could see my parachute open above me and the twists in the cords unwinding. There were two Gurkhas just above and behind me. Then as I looked down I saw that I was drifting towards the dark green jungle on the edge of the dropping zone, but after the mental effort of going through the doorway of the Dakota everything else seemed easy.

I landed upside down in some bushes on the edge of a stream that ran along the eastern edge of the paddy field. I could see Karens running across the paddy towards me as I went into the bushes. I turned the quick release and struck the catch with the palm of my hand so that the harness fell away. Then I removed the little blue bag around my neck, made sure that the Colt .45 automatic that I carried was still in the shoulder holster under my left armpit and scrambled up the bank in time to see the Dakota making another circle, to drop the second stick. All the Gurkhas in my own stick were distributed along the paddy field in a long line and were busy disentangling themselves from their harness. When they were joined in the course of a few seconds by the second stick an animated debate commenced in which every one was attempting to describe and demonstrate to every one else just how he had landed. In the midst of this I found myself carrying on a conversation in a mixture of Burmese and English with the local headman, a quick nervous young Karen with beautiful dark brown eyes that roved the landscape uncertainly while he spoke.

His English was about as fluent as my Burmese, which was not in itself adequate to prolonged negotiations. Fortunately we were soon joined by the Burma Signals Naik Chaung Waung who was a Chin and the Karen signalman Nya Mein. Chaung Waung spoke fluent English and Burmese and Nya Mein spoke fluent Burmese and Karen. So between the three of us we could interrogate the headman. At the time of my briefing I had been told that my destination was Pyagawpu, where I was to rendezvous with Jerry Hayter, who was jumping from another aeroplane, and with Guthrie who was in charge of the levies on the spot. I asked after Guthrie and then after the *thakin* with the damaged foot in case his name should not be known to them. There was no sign of Jerry, who should theoretically have arrived before my party.

After a certain amount of rather laboured interpretation it transpired that we were not at Pyagawpu at all, but at a village called Lipeykhi about four hours' march to the north-west. I

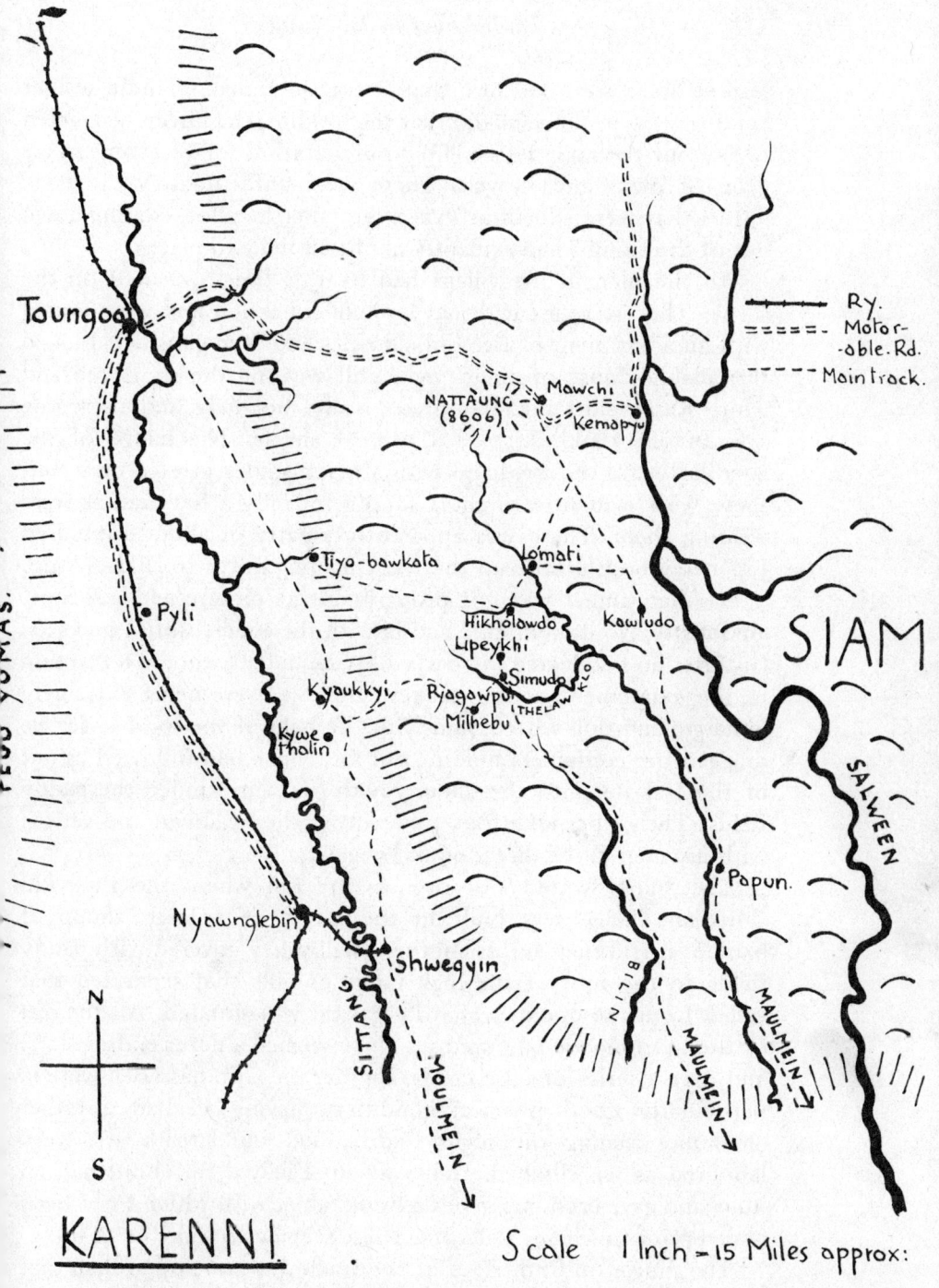

Toungoo

NATTAUNG
(8606)
Mawchi
Kemapyu

Tiyo-bawkata

Lomati

Pyli

Hikholowdo
Lipeykhi
Kawludo

SIAM

Kyaukkyi
Pyagawpu
Simudo
THELAW

Kywe
tholin

Milhebu

Papun.

Nyawngkbin

Shwegyin

SALWEEN

BILIN

MAULMEIN

MAULMEIN

MOULMEIN

SITTANG

PEGU YOMAS.

N

S

Ry.
Motor-
-able Rd.
Main track.

KARENNI

Scale   1 Inch = 15 Miles approx:

learned later from Guthrie that it was intended to build a light landing strip in the area and that the headman had been instructed to lay out the code letters TW in preparation for receiving an air drop of picks and shovels. These were unfortunately the same letters that were shown at Pyagawpu, and the pilot, coming down out of the clouds, had evidently confused the two places.

All the men in the village had by this time appeared on the scene. They were a cut-throat looking collection and were armed with an assortment of Lee Enfield rifles and Sten guns that looked formidable. Most of them were still wearing the short red and white Karen shirt manufactured locally, but here and there one saw an old khaki shirt or a pair of shorts. The badge of the guerillas was a red armband with a black spider printed on it, but these were evidently in short supply for only a few Karens were wearing them. There was apparently a party of about a hundred Japanese about a mile up the track leading north to Hikholawdo.

At that time I was not properly in the picture and was most anxious to avoid premature action with the enemy until I had seen Guthrie. So I collected my party of parachutists who, as a reaction to the excitement of the last few minutes, were being extremely lethargic and dull-witted, and with the help of the local levies we dragged the containers holding our kit, which had followed us out of the Dakota, into the undergrowth that surrounded the paddy fields. Then I bespoke four guides from the headman and set off with my men in the direction of Pyagawpu.

The track wound east over a tiny hill where the Lipeykhi Christian village was built in the midst of a large clump of bamboos, and then across another small valley covered with paddy fields to the foot of the high range of hills that separated that valley from the one in which Pyagawpu was situated. All the rest of the morning we laboured up what seemed a never ending slope and over a series of false crests. Neither the Gurkhas nor I were in particularly good physical condition, having all had a rather alcoholic evening the night before, and our breath was very laboured as we climbed. Half way up I halted for about half an hour and gave each man a benzedrine tablet with which I had been issued prior to leaving Calcutta. These seemed to wake us all up.

The jungle on both sides of the track was more open than that in the Manipur hills above Imphal and it looked as if cross-country movement was possible without cutting. There did not appear to be any teak, but on the lower slopes of the mountains there was a great deal of bamboo. The sun grew very hot as we neared the top of the range which was about 4,500 feet above sea level and on the other side one caught a very beautiful glimpse of Mount Plakho across the next valley.

We descended abruptly about 2,000 feet until the path crossed a clear mountain stream where we halted to quench our thirst. Then we continued on about a quarter of a mile to the village of Takokodo with the track crossing the stream by means of little bridges of bamboo every fifty or sixty yards. Here our guides evidently had friends, and Nya Mein, the Karen from the Burma Signals, asked if we would like food. Both my men and I were by that time ravenously hungry, and we did ample justice to the very appetising dish of pork and rice that was put before us. Afterwards the going was much easier as we followed the valley south towards the Thelaw Klo which is a stream running west to east towards the Yunzalin Chaung, which intersects the valley at Pyagawpu.

Pyagawpu was in fact not nearly such a large village as it appeared to be on the map where it was shown in large letters. It was rather more of an administrative centre for a whole group of less well known villages in the surrounding hills than a centre of population in its own right. It boasted a police station, a school and a church and was surrounded by a wide cultivated area of paddy fields containing a great many huts on stilts which were occupied in the rainy season when the villagers came down from the surrounding hill villages to plant the rice crop and again during the harvest time. The village itself consisted of about half a dozen huts lying just north of the Thelaw Klo. Just beyond it was Guthrie's camp in an old paddy hut on the edge of the jungle. Jerry had arrived that morning.

Guthrie was an imposing figure with a gigantic spade shaped beard that made him look like Robinson Crusoe. His leg had set at an angle and he could only hobble about slowly with the aid of a long bamboo stick. He must have suffered very much while he was hiding on the mountain. I never saw him without his beard and so my impressions are probably quite different from what they would have been if I had met him in a civilised area. To me there was something very biblical about Guthrie and I should never have been surprised if he had suddenly embarked upon a long religious dissertation. All the Karens said that he was growing to look very like Seagrim, and he was an object of great respect.

Prior to this operation Guthrie had tried his hand at most things. He had flouted a parental wish that he should become a merchant banker in the City at a very early age, and had at one time and another been actor, journalist, playwright and novelist. When the war broke out he had gone to Finland to enlist in a British volunteer group to fight against the Russians, and when that war had come to an end he had only escaped by the skin of his teeth by pretending that he was an American citizen and getting himself evacuated with their nationals to the United States. Once there he had succeeded in slipping across the border into Canada, but even then his troubles had not been over, as he was still guilty of offences under the Canadian immigration regulations.

In the end the easiest way to get back to England had been to enlist in the Canadian Army, and with them he had returned as a sergeant. Guthrie had been very happy in that capacity and it had come as something of a shock when he was recommended for a commission. To begin with he had argued that, as a Britisher, his position would be an invidious one if he were to be commissioned in the Canadian Army. But it had been at a time when there was an acute officer shortage, and he had finally transferred back to the British Army and been commissioned into the DCLI. At D-Day Guthrie had gone into the Maquis in France and done much the same type of work that he was doing in Karenni in a European setting.

Guthrie's companions on the mountain had been Sergeant Moore, a Shan called Ludan and the one armed headman of the Pyagawpu village group. Prior to the operation there had been a general request throughout South East Asia Command for wireless operators to volunteer as parachutists. There had been very little response to this call, and Sergeant Moore had been one of the very few to come forward. He was an excellent type of fellow to have as an operator on such an operation. Although not particularly tough nor particularly sure of himself in the role of guerilla—parachutist, he had all the Londoner's charm and ability to take people and situations as they came and was a great favourite with the locals. When I met him he also had a large black spade shaped beard, which in conjunction with a pair of steel rimmed Army issue spectacles gave him the appearance of a foreign professor of botany.

The headman lived in Papun in peacetime, and had only been elected to his office in Pyagawpu since the Japanese invasion. He was a great stalwart of the Baptist Church and insisted on Guthrie and Sergeant Moore attending the service with him on Sundays. He spoke ungrammatical English and had been to school in Rangoon. While he was there he had been knocked over by a tram and had lost an arm.

After Guthrie had returned to the valley he had been supplied with a wireless set by the area commander who was over in the foothills near to the Sittang and had taken several air drops of arms and ammunition. After the departure of the Japanese battalion which had come up to investigate the original report of parachutists, the Pyagawpu area had been very peaceful, and it was the colonel's intention to build it up into a firm base in which to establish a permanent headquarters. Guthrie had recruited a force of mobile levies in the area, and I learned from Jerry, who had arrived that morning, that I was to take them over and run the district.

Shortly after the arrival of Turrall's party at Pyagawpu a message had been received from Saw Thet Wa, Seagrim's original wireless operator, who had been missing since the time when Seagrim surrendered and the local Karen leaders were rounded up by the Japanese and taken away to Rangoon. He had been tried at the same time as Seagrim and afterwards imprisoned in the gaol at Rangoon, where he had been underfed and often beaten up. Together with some American airmen he had made plans to escape, but these had been discovered and for some time he had been under threat of execution. Then the Japanese had shown a change of policy towards the Karens and his life had been spared.

The Japanese had received a great deal of help from the

Burmese at the time of their invasion and to begin with treated them as a favoured race in the country. But when the Burmese had realised that their new masters were not quite the charming fellow-Buddhists that they had at first thought them to be and started to show signs of unrest, there was an abrupt change of face and the Japanese had attempted to cultivate the loyalty of the Karens and Shans. Saw Thet Wa probably owed his life to this change of attitude on the part of the Japanese. They had removed him from the Rangoon prison, and set him to work as a cook-interpreter in the *Kempei Tai* Headquarters.

Shortly after Turrall's arrival in Karenni the particular unit with which Saw Thet Wa was working was sent off to Papun and thence it went up into the Pyagawpu area. He contrived to send off a message to Turrall when on his way to Lipeykhi and the headman had arranged an ambush. Saw Thet Wa was wearing Japanese uniform at the time and made desperate efforts to separate from his Japanese companions as the party neared the place where he knew the ambush was laid. But the *Kempei Tai* must have had their suspicions of Saw Thet Wa, for they steadfastly refused to let him out of their sight. When the ambush was sprung he was standing in the midst of the party, but luck was on his side and he escaped unhurt. Three Japanese were killed at the ambush and the only survivor to escape into the jungle was later waylaid and killed on the road to Papun. Saw Thet Wa rejoined the levies and was living at Guthrie's camp when I arrived. He was a tall Karen from the Delta who spoke almost perfect English. He had very obviously had a rough time during the years of his captivity.

A few hours before I reached Pyagawpu another British officer called Wilson who had originally been operating with Turrall in the foothills east of the Sittang came into camp. He was a good-looking young man who had been a commercial artist before the war, and he ran his levies on very regimental lines. At that time there were two systems on which levies might be enlisted. The older men with families to look after and fields to cultivate were on the whole not disposed to travel far from their villages, but were willing enough to join in the war if it approached their own homes. They were therefore enlisted as static levies. This meant that they were given a weapon and ammunition and allowed to live in their own homes where they worked under the control of a local leader appointed to control that particular district.

Some of the younger men and boys were willing enough to enlist on terms more like those applying to regular soldiers and to move around the countryside with a particular British Officer. They came to be known as mobile levies. In addition, there were of course the Special Groups of parachutists who had come in as a nucleus of trained men to stiffen the levies. Turrall had brought in a Special Group with him that had been recruited in Burma and trained in the use of explosives. My Special Group was made up from the Assam Rifles that had been training with V Force in Shillong. They were regular soldiers, and had volunteered for the operation, but they had not previously received training in explosives and did not speak Burmese. Nevertheless with the natural bonhomie of the Gurkha, who is very similar to the British soldier in his ability to get along with and endear himself to foreign peoples, they were soon enough fraternising with the Karen levies in a weird language of signs and garbled Karen and Burmese words. Guthrie gave them some instruction in the use of explosives and they became tremendously enthusiastic.

In the morning I started the mobile levies that Guthrie had recruited training with the Gurkhas, but at about ten o'clock there was a report that a hundred Japanese were in the area of a little village called Pomuda somewhere on the top of the range that I had crossed the day before on my way from Lipeykhi. This was very obviously the same party that had been in Lipeykhi and Jerry at once ordered out Wilson's levies and my own to take up a ring of ambush positions on all the tracks approaching Pyagawpu. This was the first time that I had faced a dispirited Japanese force that was likely to withdraw if fired upon, and both the Ghurkhas and I were a little sceptical at the idea. But at that time such was the disorganisation among the enemy who had withdrawn from Meiktila and Central Burma that a small show of force along a particular track would more often than not deter them from using it.

I spent the night beside the track along which I had come from Lipeykhi the previous day with six of the Gurkhas and about twenty levies. The only levy among them that spoke any English was a young fellow called Saw Bla Baw, who had come in from the area east of the Yunzalin Chaung the previous day to enlist. His father was a very important headman in the area called Saw Digay, who was himself absolutely illiterate but who had sent his son down to the Government School in Papun. In the evening he asked me whether he could join my organisation as a permanent interpreter when we left Pyagawpu, and I took him on. No Japanese came in the night and about noon the following day I returned to camp. While I was drinking a cup of tea in Guthrie's hut, however, several shots rang out from the direction south of the Thelaw Klo, and Jerry and Guthrie, who had had a more comfortable night than I had, went off to investigate with a few levies.

After they had gone I felt that perhaps I had been a little lacking in enthusiasm, so I put on my shoulder holster, seized my carbine and set off along the track which they had followed. I caught up with Jerry on the north bank of the Thelaw Klo. He was questioning the Baptist padre of Pyagawpu, who had apparently seen Japanese moving south through the jungle to the west, and opened fire. The padre was quite convinced that he had inflicted a casualty, and amused me very much by announcing that when he shot the Jap 'he cried out lovely'.

Two days later Jerry decided to move the entire camp onto a new site that the villagers had been building on Mount Plakho. Guthrie's position in the valley at Pyagawpu was not suitable for a permanent headquarters as it was very close to the main track, and would have been quite untenable if large organised bodies of Japanese had started to appear in the neighbourhood. Mount Plakho, on the other hand, was in a very remote and inaccessible position.

By this time there was a considerable bulk of stores in Guthrie's camp, so that the move could not be effected all at once. We called for elephants and drivers from all the neighbouring villages, and moved a little each day. Wilson never went up to the new camp, but set off in the direction of Kawludo on the other side of the Yunzalin Chaung. At that time Hyena area had only one guerilla party under a Karen officer called Bachit operating near the Salween River, and reports from both Otter area to the north

and Mongoose area to the south suggested that the track running
north to south from Kemapyu to Papun was becoming a main
escape route for the Japanese still north of the Mawchi road.
Before he left Wilson amused us all intensely by holding a very
regimental pay parade for his levies. As he gave each man his pay
the fellow would step forward and salute in the best prescribed
military manner. One of them excelled himself by appearing
before Wilson with a little white jungle flower pinned onto his cap.

After Wilson's men had gone it was decided that I should move
with my levies to Lipeykhi, which appeared to be the only place in
the whole area where a light landing strip seemed possible. Colonel
Howell, the area commander, was moving over from the Sittang
foothills as soon as certain Japanese concentrations between his
area and Pyagawpu dispersed, and Jerry felt that Guthrie should
be evacuated before the monsoon, which was due to start at the
beginning of June.

The villagers did not start to work in the fields until after the monsoon had begun, so that there was plenty of labour available to work on the landing strip at Lipyekhi. None of us had ever done work of this kind before, but I assumed that it was just a question of flattening the little dykes that separated the different rice fields and helped to contain the water during the rainy season when the paddy was growing. There was a ditch running across the site from north-west to south-east which we filled in very laboriously with the turf that we removed from the *bands*. While we were doing this there was an early rain storm and the portion that we had filled in sank about a foot in the middle and was very soft on top. We kept carrying more earth to the spot in bamboo baskets and piling it onto the top, but the level kept sinking. In one corner of the field there was a buffalo lick, but I decided to leave that as it was.

In order to mark the edges of the landing strip the Gurkhas squashed large pieces of bamboo and then opened them up so that the inside part which was milk white was facing upwards and reflected the sun. We laid a line of these all round the strip, but kept having to replace them every few days as the inside of the bamboo lost its pristine whiteness very rapidly when exposed.

I calculated that the aeroplane would have to approach up the valley from north to south and take off in the same direction from which it came in. By cutting down a few clumps of bamboo we were able to give the pilot a fairly clear route into the strip. There was also a lemon tree near to the bamboo but the Lipeykhi villagers begged me not to cut it down and I had not the heart to do so. At the south end of the strip the valley came to an end and the hills rose too steeply for an aeroplane to take off with any safety. The specifications given in a book that I had with me required the strip to be at least six hundred yards long. This particular strip was a bare five hundred, but when I exchanged notes with Jerry on the subject he reckoned it would be all right. Actually, when the first Lysander landed it came to a standstill in little over two hundred yards.

The Lipeykhi villagers were at first a little nervous about commencing work, as they said that if the Japanese found the strip they would take punitive measures against the village. I promised to remain with the Gurkhas and protect them and this seemed to reassure them, a fact which made me feel rather guilty as I knew that my chances of holding the place against an organised Jap force were slight.

The Lipeykhi villagers were partly Christian and partly animist and lived in separate villages according to their beliefs. In addition to the headman who I had met when I landed, there was an English-speaking schoolmaster who was very helpful. His sideline was the capturing and taming of wild elephants, and in peacetime an expedition had departed from the village every year to the Pegu Yomas for this purpose. In spite of their being skilled in such a dangerous occupation, the villagers were not on the whole a warlike bunch and had not nearly such a good static levy or Home Guard organisation as the smaller villages of Hikholawdo and Tibawkhi to the north.

One of the biggest personalities in the area was a very distinguished looking old gentleman called Saw Ja Po, who was invariably immaculately dressed in a pair of khaki shorts and shirt. He had formerly been the headman himself, but had retired before the war as he considered himself too old. Nevertheless he was still a tower of strength, and invariably appeared beside the Gurkhas with a rifle whenever there was talk of Japanese in the area.

To begin with only the men from the village appeared in the area of the paddy hut where the Gurkhas and I were living during the building of the landing strip. Then one day the headman and the schoolmaster brought their wives down to call, and after that our camp became a regular haunt for the women and children during the mornings. I was always a little afraid that one day I should learn that one of the Gurkhas had seduced a local beauty, but no such incident occurred. In fact after a few weeks the Karens had accepted the Gurkhas as their own.

We had already collected one escaped Gurkha prisoner of war

in the Pyagawpu area. His battalion had suffered heavily in the Moulmein area during the original Burma retreat and he had escaped into the hills and joined up with Seagrim. He had been in Japanese hands twice, and his nerves were in bad condition. I evacuated him on a Lysander as soon as the landing strip started to operate.

One day Saw Pathaw, the commander of the static levies in the Hikholawdo area, came to see me. He was a Karen Baptist padre who spoke very good English and had already on two occasions engaged parties of Japanese that had passed near to his village. He had just received information that a party of some thirty of the enemy was making its way towards Siam through the hills and was due in the area of Hikholawdo the following day. I sent up Rabe Thapa, one of the Gurkha Lance-Naiks, with a section of the mobile levies and four other Assam Riflemen, and they did an ambush the next night. Not more than two Japs were killed in the ambush, but the whole party became separated into groups of two and three which were easy game for the static levies during the next few days. I was glad that Rabe Thapa had been able to start off with an easy ambush, as he had had a difficult time on the Chindwin with 3 V Ops in the early days of the war, and it had had the effect of making him credit the enemy with a supernatural cunning that they did not really possess.

Guthrie arrived on an elephant the day before the first Lysander was due to come. But the weather deteriorated the following day, and we waited in vain. After that each day meant that the monsoon was a little nearer and I began to wonder whether Guthrie would ever get away. I suppose the same thoughts were passing through Guthrie's mind as well, but he never for one moment gave voice to them.

Then two days later Colonel Howell, the Hyene area commander, himself arrived from the Pada Chaung with a French Canadian officer called Fournier, a wireless operator called Sergeant Rowe and about a dozen Karens en route for Mount Plakho. He was a good looking energetic man who looked much younger than his forty years. His life had been a very adventurous one. Starting off as a midshipman in the Royal Navy in the First World War, he had gone on to serve as a pilot in the Royal

At Mount Plakho Headquarters: Corporal Storrie, myself, and Sergeant Moore with Sergeant Rowe and Saw San Sein behind

The Hyena Area Headquarters staff

Canadian Air Force and as an executive in a coal mining venture in China. For a few glorious months he had even been a czar of the milk retail trade in Shanghai but this brief reign had come to an end when the Japanese had moved in. He had been a staff officer on Wingate's Second Chindit operation, and was a very good organiser. His knowledge of flying was of considerable value in adding the finishing touches to the landing strip.

Late that afternoon when the ceiling was very low and we had quite given up hope that the Lysander would come we heard an aeroplane engine overhead. For a few agonising minutes it circled out of sight, and then as a great crowd of Karens started to gather from all directions it finally appeared out of the clouds.

Having circled twice it came in to land, and my heart was in my mouth as the wheels first grounded, but the pilot made a perfect landing and pulled up with two hundred yards to spare. He had been searching the hills for five hours and must have only found the place by chance in that weather. He was a young Flight Sergeant new to Burma called Castledine and was very tired but exceedingly pleased that he had arrived. He reckoned that now he would know how to find the landing strip whenever called upon to do so. I envied Guthrie when he went off to civilisation.

The same day just as darkness was falling a Karen arrived outside my paddy hut with news that two Japanese prisoners were being brought into camp. His companions had been afraid that if they had arrived in the half darkness the Gurkhas might have taken them for an enemy party and opened fire. The Colonel was very excited about the news as up till that time no prisoners had been taken in the operation and now that the light landing strip was working it would be possible to evacuate them.

The Japanese were brought in about twenty minutes later and I met them on the edge of the paddy field and then took them over to the hut where the Colonel was sleeping. Both of them were naked except for loin cloths and I think that they thought they were about to die. They bowed very ceremoniously when they saw me.

In the Colonel's hut we gave them each a blanket to put over their shoulders and set about interrogating them with the assistance of Padu, the Colonel's interpreter, and a pamphlet entitled *Notes for Forward Units on the Japanese Army*, which contained a long list of questions such as 'What is your name?' 'What unit do you come from?' etc., written in Japanese characters. Padu was a Karen from Toungoo, who had been an inspector of education under the puppet regime and spoke a little Japanese. He had fled into the hills and joined the guerillas when the British started to advance. He managed to ask a good many of our questions for us, and when he was at a loss we would point at the Japanese version of the question in the pamphlet and then get the prisoner to write down the answer on a piece of paper.

One of them was a Corporal in a Japanese motor transport section attached to an Indian National Army unit. The other was a first class private in the infantry. After they learned that they were not going to be executed, they showed not the slightest hesitation in answering our questions. They had been in a hospital in Central Burma when the Fourteenth Army had broken down the main road to Rangoon, and together they had set off to walk to Siam. They had crossed the Sittang with some other hospital patients north of Kyaukkyi, but the party had been ambushed by guerillas in the Pada Valley, which was one of the main entrances to the foothills. Both of them had round cheerful Mongolian faces and the Colonel, who was in certain respects an admirer of the Japanese race, gave orders for them to be fed and housed for the night and evacuated to Rangoon by Lysander. This decision was certainly not popular with the Gurkhas and Karens, who believed that the only good kind of Japanese was a dead one.

In the morning the Colonel and his party set off for main headquarters on Mount Plakho. It had rained a good deal during the night and the surface of the landing strip had deteriorated badly. The Gurkhas built a bamboo cell for the Japanese prisoners among the stilts of the paddy hut in which we lived. Every time I passed them they bowed very politely. In the evening another prisoner was brought in. He was a second class private from the field artillery and looked very surprised when he saw his two compatriots solemnly partaking of a curry meal from British issue mess tins in the bamboo cage beneath the hut. The Gurkhas were not particularly happy when he arrived, and it was a great drain on my very small manpower to have three sentries posted over the prisoners day and night.

Now that Guthrie was evacuated I decided to move north with a small party to Hikholawdo and thence to Lomati to reconnoitre the ground and establish contact with the local leaders. Apart from the Japanese who were still west of the Sittang, there were large concentrations on the Mawchi-Kemapyu road and in the Loikaw area, and as all available information seemed to suggest that they were not using the direct routes across the upper Salween to Siam, but making their way south through Papun and then crossing the river in its lower reaches in the vicinity of Moulmein, it seemed very likely that I might one day have to give battle in and around Lomati and Hikholawdo.

Among my Gurkhas I had three NCOs. Havildar Bom Bahadur Gurung was a well educated Darjeeling Gurkha, who was rather more intelligent than the general run of his race, and very brave withal. I decided to leave him behind on the landing strip to supervise the arrival of any further aeroplanes that might come in and to look after the prisoners. I also left Lance-Naik Rabe Thapa as he was suffering from malaria and was not nearly such a good operational NCO as Lance-Naik Man Bahadur. Man Bahadur was a Chettri, and the best fighting soldier in my group. Although he had thirteen years' service, he had only just been awarded his first stripe. Not very intelligent, he was a hard NCO and not really at his best in command of levies as he did not understand the rather free and easy type of discipline that was necessary. But one knew instinctively that he would be a magnificent person to have beside one in a fight.

I had not intended that our expedition to Lomati should be an offensive one, but when the time came to set forth in the morning I found that Man Bahadur had armed the section of mobile levies that was to accompany us with two Bren guns and that he had also chosen three of the best Assam Riflemen. These were a very tall Thapa called Gopal Singh who invariably wore a cheerful grin, on his face; a minute little fellow called Surabdhau Rai, who looked about fourteen years old and was always busy taking the mechanism of obscure weapons to pieces and as often as not finding that he was unable to put them together again; and

Jamkholem Kuki, who was not a Gurkha at all but an excellent soldier all the same.

Hikholawdo is only about two hours' march up the main track leading north from Lipeykhi. One climbs for a while after one leaves the village until one crosses a pass at about 3,000 feet above sea level by the village of Balawkhi and then falls abruptly towards a *chaung* rising in the watershed to the west above the Sittang and flowing north east into the Yunzalin Chaung. Hikholawdo is or was a spotlessly clean village with a charming little Baptist Church and a fine light guest house in which we left our packs after we arrived. It stands on the hillside above the *chaung* with the mountain stretching up behind it to the south. All the rice fields are north of the village and on the other side of the *chaung*, and beyond them the mountains rise again very precipitously on the way to the Mawchi road.

Shortly after our arrival a runner came in with a message from Havildar Bom Bahadur at Lipeykhi to the effect that villagers from the west reported a force of about thee hundred Japs moving towards the Yunzalin from the direction of the Pada Chaung. Hardly had I finished reading it, when a stream of women and children started to come up the hill from the Hikholawdo paddy fields with the news that a party of twelve Japanese had come down the track from the west and were cooking rice in a paddy hut on the northern side of the *chaung*.

I gathered my section of mobile levies and Saw Bla Baw and with Man Bahadur and the Gurkhas hurried down the hill to the southern bank of the stream. It was about twenty-five yards wide and was not more than two feet deep at its deepest point in that season. There seemed to be two well defined crossing places from which tracks ran up into the village. I left Man Bahadur, Gopal Singh and Jamkholem Kuki with five levies and a Bren gun watching the one and took up a position covering the other with Surabdhau Rai, Saw Bla Baw and another five mobile levies. That was at about five o'clock.

From the top of the hill above Hikholawdo the villagers could see the paddy fields. The padre Saw Pathaw sent me down a message at nightfall that as yet no more Japanese had joined the first party. He suggested going across the *chaung* and attacking the hut in which they were cooking, but I have always made it a fundamental rule of work with levies that one only fights when one has contrived to get into a better position than one's opponent and I had no desire to engage in a dog fight with a Japanese force of unknown strength at nightfall in an area that my men had not reconnoitred.

It was then at the very peak of a moon period, and after the sun had set we had clear visibility across the *chaung*. After I had thought about the ground a little, I made up my mind that if the Japanese decided to go to Hikholawdo they would use the path that Man Bahadur's party were watching. So I closed my own party on to his and we withdrew a little into the bushes so that we were less likely to be seen by anybody approaching the *chaung* from the opposite direction. Saw Pathaw brought us down a very good dish of curry in the evening, and after that I posted sentries and settled down to wait. There was one short burst of light automatic fire from the paddy field during the night which as an isolated sound in the silence was very eery, but apart from that all was quiet. I experienced an almost insufferable desire to drop off to sleep during the night, but with badly trained levies around me I could not rely on the sentries' remaining awake.

After dawn Saw Pathaw sent down another levy with a message to the effect that the paddy fields had filled with Japanese during the night. On the other side of the *chaung* there was a stretch of undergrowth before the fields started which prevented my party from seeing them. I knew that the next two or three hours was the dangerous period. Japanese troops on the march forage from village to village as they move, and after a long night march parties would probably scatter in search of food.

We were all very tired after our night on the river bank which had been infested with mosquitoes, but our vigil was rewarded about an hour later. Suddenly I felt Man Bahadur stiffen beside me, and there sure enough was a party of some thirty Japanese soldiers moving down the track towards the *chaung* in single file. In that moment I understood something of the thrill of big game hunting. We waited until the leading Japanese was half way across the chaung and then Man Bahadur opened fire. The first burst from the Bren gun seemed to cause the leading trio of Japanese to disintegrate. Then as the remainder darted to right and left of the track and the target grew wider and less concentrated Gopal Singh's Bren opened up and another little group of khaki-clad Japanese seemed to melt away in the middle of the track.

The lust for slaughter seized us all for a few seconds. I could see Surabdhau Rai, who was carrying a Sten, leap to his feet, press the change lever over to 'Rapid fire' and fire round after round into the bushes into which the Japanese had disappeared. After each round he would pause and hiss the equivalent of 'Take that, you bastards' in Gurkhali. I gave the order to withdraw.

It was a very successful and artistic little ambush and we all felt very pleased with ourselves when we reached our next position above the village. The Japanese waited about twenty minutes before they came forward to examine the scene of the ambush and bury their dead. Casualties, which numbered six, were not heavy, as the Bren gun is too accurate a weapon for such an occasion. But they had doubtless received a very unpleasant shock. They remained in the fields on the other side of the stream throughout the day and killed a buffalo and fired a mortar several times into the jungle. Then at nightfall they moved north-east in the direction of Lomati.

We returned to Lipeykhi during the afternoon to find that two Lysanders had come into the airstrip earlier in the day. The Colonel had come back from main headquarters and had been flown out in one of them to Rangoon for a conference. A very elderly Japanese with a map had been brought in at the last moment and put aboard the second plane with the other prisoners just as it was taking off. There was also a message from Jerry at Mount Plakho to warn us that the Colonel would be returning from Rangoon in the morning.

While we were drinking a cup of tea just after our arrival Saw Bla Baw appeared with the news that a hundred Japs were descending the hill into the Lipeykhi paddy fields from the direction of a little mountain village called Bikodo on the watershed to the west. Havildar Bom Bahadur paraded the levy section that had not accompanied me to Hikholawdo the previous day and the remaining Gurkhas and went off to lay an ambush at

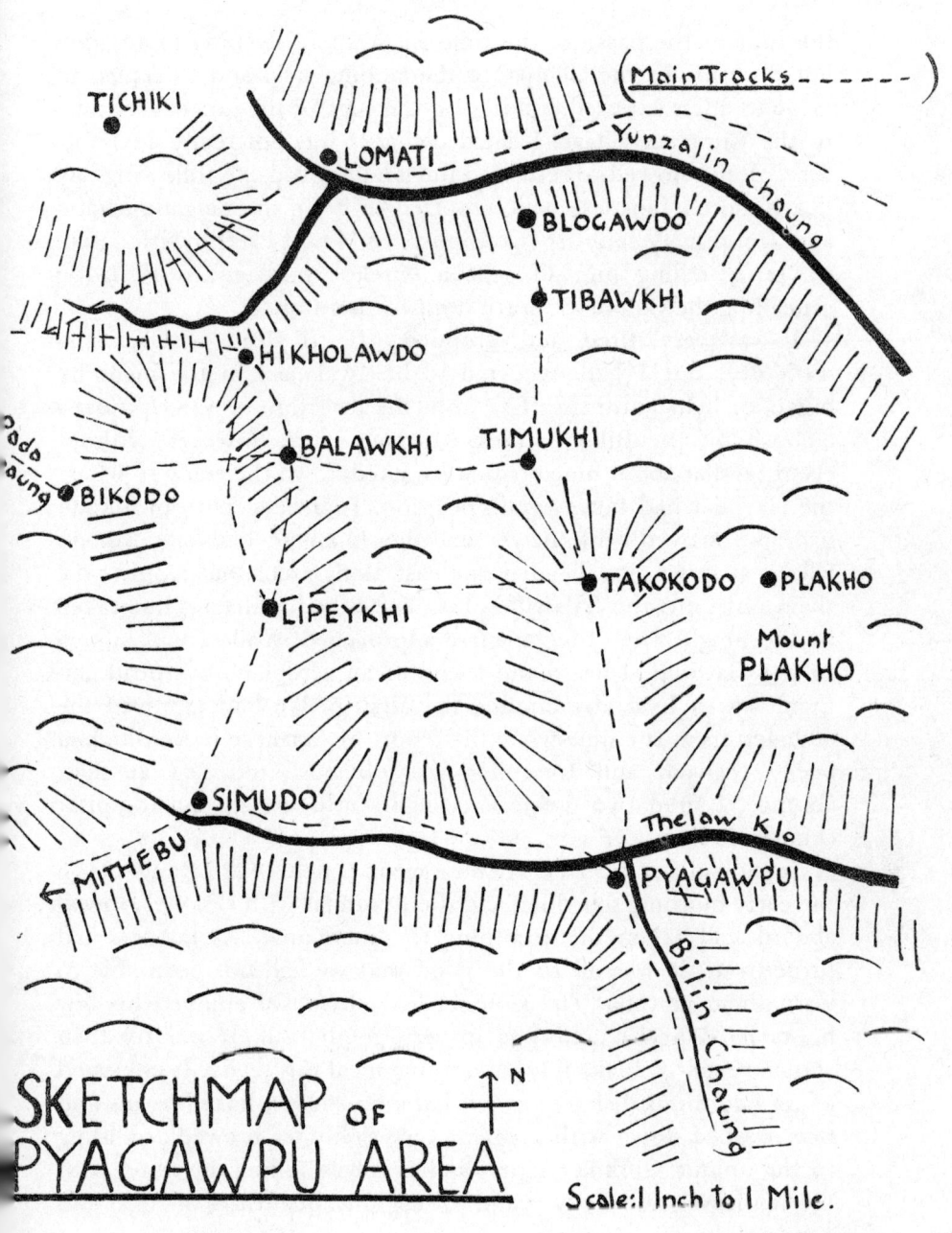

TICHIKI

(Main Tracks ------)

LOMATI

Yunzalin Chaung

BLOGAWDO

TIBAWKHI

HIKHOLAWDO

Dodo Chaung

BIKODO

BALAWKHI

TIMUKHI

LIPEYKHI

TAKOKODO ●PLAKHO

Mount
PLAKHO

SIMUDO

Thelaw Klo

MITHEBU

PYAGAWPU

Bilin Chaung

SKETCHMAP OF PYAGAWPU AREA

↑N

Scale: 1 Inch to 1 Mile.

the foot of the pass. At the time we were all sleeping in a paddy hut on stilts in the vicinity of the landing strip and I decided to move to a less exposed building on the edge of the jungle very near to the Christian village. I decided that it was not really advisable for Colonel Howell to return to the landing strip the following day if a hundred Japanese were reported to be in the neighbourhood and accordingly sent off two runners to Mount Plakho with a note to Jerry telling him to sent a wireless message to Rangoon cancelling the Colonel's return until further notice.

I was very tired and dropped off to sleep without any difficulty, but I half expected to be awakened in the night by bursts of light automatic fire from the direction of the Havildar's ambush on the Bikodo track. Morning came, however, without event, and at about nine o'clock I walked down the track to where the Havildar had taken up his position. Two villagers from Bikodo had just arrived with news that the Japanese had left Bikodo village at dawn and headed due east along a col that would take them out onto the Balawkhi pass. The Bikodo villagers had taken to the jungle when the Japanese approached. While I was talking to the Havildar, I heard the sound of an aeroplane overhead and there was a Lysander circling the airstrip. We had removed the code letters at the time when the report of Japanese in Bikodo had been received, and the pilot was obviously puzzled at their absence. I fired two green Very lights into the air and the pilot came in to land.

Jerry had not received my message in time to warn Rangoon on the early morning schedule, and the Lysander with Colonel Howell aboard had taken off according to programme. As matters had turned out, it was all to the good that we had not been able to warn them in time. The Colonel had obviously enjoyed his few hours in Rangoon and was in very good form. It was by then about eleven o'clock and the morning meal was ready. It consisted of an enormous dish of curried bamboo shoots, baked beans and rice, washed down with mugs of very sickly tea brewed according to the unique Gurkha recipe which involves boiling the water with the tea leaves already in it and adding large quantities of sugar and condensed milk.

I learned the latest news from the war. The Japanese 15th

Division, which the Gurkhas and I had known before in the Imphal battle, had apparently been ordered to fight and die on the Mawchi—Kemapyu road, and at that time the Indian 19th Division was pushing forward against them at a snail's pace. The Colonel was very angry at the decision of the higher-ups to attempt an advance along this road during the monsoon. It had a metalled surface, but wound its way into the mountains close to the Nattaung across innumerable bridges and other obstacles which gave every advantage to the defence.

During the previous fortnight it had been confirmed that the other two Japanese divisions that had attempted the invasion of Imphal in 1944, 31 and 33 Divisions, had withdrawn from Mawchi down the track leading east of the Yunzalin Chaung, through Kawludo and Papun to the coastal area around Bilin and Thaton. Bachit, the Karen officer, east of the Yunzalin, had attempted a few ambushes and been chased into the hills running just west of the Salween River. Wilson had crossed the Yunzalin due west of Kawludo, and was starting to take offensive action along the main track. North of the Mawchi road there was still a large Japanese concentration in the area of Loikaw, and all information suggested that instead of withdrawing east across the Salween in the direction of the Chiengmai railhead in Siam they would follow 31 and 33 Divisions down the Mawchi—Papun track. Food would be getting rather short along this track if it was used by further bodies of Japanese troops, and the Colonel felt that at a future date it was highly likely that parties of enemy would head southwest across the Yunzalin after reaching the Lomati area, and attempt to forage their way through Pyagawpu.

By that time all the villagers had concealed their rice stocks in little jungle caches, and only sufficient was kept in the villages to feed the inhabitants from day to day. By this means it was hoped to hamper Japanese foraging activities to a very great extent. It was still possible for a large force moving through the Karen hills to search the jungle around the Karen villages until they came upon these caches, but this was a slow process. At the time when the Japanese battalion had occupied Pyagawpu and searched the surrounding jungle for Guthrie and Moore, a patrol had moved into the Lipeykhi area and found signs of work upon what looked like a landing strip. As a punitive measure they had therefore burned the Lipeykhi rice stocks. This had meant that the Lipeykhi villagers had started the year with a shortage and that by that time the existing stocks were practically exhausted. The Colonel had therefore arranged for two Dakota loads of rice to be dropped in the area in the near future to supply the villagers until their next crop was available in December.

The Karen villagers have a particularly terrifying way of saying 'Japan', emphasising the final syllable. While the Colonel was talking I heard this particular intonation being placed upon the word down in the levies' side of the hut, and decided that there was trouble afoot. Sure enough Saw Bla Baw came hurrying over a minute later with the information that Kabukhi village was surrounded by Japanese. Kabukhi village was a group of houses a little north of the Lipeykhi animist village.

I took out a party with the two-inch mortar with the intention of putting down a bomb somewhere in the vicinity of the enemy in the hope of frightening them away. I felt that they would regard a mortar as a very sophisticated weapon rather beyond the intelligence of mere guerillas and imagine that they were up against regular parachute troops. The ground was, however, not suitable for my plan, and by the time that I reached a point from which it would have been possible for me to fire, there was a crowd of Karen women and children passing across the fields in front of me. The Japanese had apparently come into the village very quickly and withdrawn after a most perfunctory search for rice in the houses. We returned to the paddy hut on the edge of the jungle by the air strip. It was by then about five o'clock.

When I had fired the green Very light and gone down to meet the Colonel on the landing strip, I had left Lance-Naik Rabe Thapa and five levies up on the track leading to Bikodo where the Havildar's party had spent the night. Shortly after five o'clock two of these levies had decided that they had no more to fear from the enemy for that day at any rate, and taken it into their heads to walk across some open ground to a small stream. Suddenly three shots were fired at them from the jungle that ran down from the col between Bikodo and Balawkhi to the edge of the paddy fields.

News of this incident arrived just after I had returned from my rather abortive attempt to mortar the enemy in Kabukhi village, and after a day of alarums and excursions it irritated me a great deal. Havildar Bom Bahadur took out Rabe Thapa and the two inch mortar, crept up to position from which he could overlook the point from which the enemy had fired, and discharged three bombs into the jungle behind.

The Colonel and I spent an uneasy night on the floor of my headquarters hut, but there were no further incidents to disturb us. In the morning the headman and the schoolmaster came over from the Christian village to report that the local scouts could find no trace of the enemy in the areas where they had been the previous evening. The Colonel waited until about ten o'clock and then decided that it was safe to continue his journey to Mount Plakho. He passed through Takokodo just after the same party of Japanese had bypassed the village. The headman had borrowed a Bren gun from main headquarters and given them a very brisk welcome. They had scattered into the jungle, crossed the valley onto the lower slopes of Mount Plakho a little further to the south and then headed due east up the hill. At that time Jerry was away from headquarters and there was only the Bengali doctor, De Wanjea, and two British wireless operators with a handful of mobile levies in the place. The Japanese had followed a jungle track that might well have taken them out in the midst of the wireless huts, but they had fortunately turned right before they reached the top of the mountain and followed a path leading south.

4

It was after the regular troops crossed the Sittang River at Shwegyin that the Japanese on the east bank in the area between Kyaukkyi and Toungoo started to come up into the mountains. Before that they had been moving down the road through the plains without entering the guerilla area except in isolated small parties. Fortunately for us they were nearly always badly armed and in an advanced state of exhaustion, and their only thought was to escape across the Salween into Siam.

After the monsoon broke at the beginning of June movement across country in the plains became very difficult. Small streams that were only several inches deep during the dry season rose to six feet or more. They started to flow very swiftly and the bamboo bridges that had spanned them during the summer were carried away in the spate. The paddy fields began to fill with water and the villagers settled down to the task of ploughing up the ground with their slow patient water-buffaloes and planting the paddy in the mud.

In the hills movement across country was a little easier. The water drained off the mountain slopes and there was not the same thick layer of mud on the paths, that one found in the plains. Provided that one had a good set of nails in one's boots one could move along at a fair pace. And although the *chaungs* ran more swiftly, it was always possible to make a detour up the hill side until one reached a point above their source.

In the jungle there were many leeches and on the march these would fasten themselves to one's boots and crawl upwards onto one's legs. It was necessary to brush them off at once before they had had time to embed their fangs. Otherwise their removal left a tiny sore which bled persistently. There were two schools of thought in the jungle regarding the leech problem. If one wore long trousers it was possible to bind the bottoms of them to the tops of one's boots with a pair of puttees in such a way as to provide little loophole for a leech to penetrate. But on the march the puttees were bound to work themselves loose, and once a leech was inside one had no means of removing it until one finally made a long halt and was able to carry out a thorough inspection. By then it was usually so swollen with blood that it was ready to drop off of its own accord.

On the other hand, if one wore a pair of shorts, although it was impossible to prevent a leech from crawling over the tops of one's boots and onto one's legs, one could at any rate see at a glance the moment it was there and remove it with the blade of a knife before it had a chance to get its teeth embedded.

During the monsoon the leeches made sleeping out in the jungle at night very unpleasant. For some unknown reason they rarely if ever penetrated into a village or other inhabited area, and one therefore contrived to sleep under cover wherever possible. When it was really necessary to bivouac in the open it was advisable to lay oneself down on the site of a fire or in the vicinity of fresh running water. Leeches always avoided flame and the ashes that remained after a fire had died down, and the quickest way of removing one that was attached was to apply a lighted cigarette end to its head. Although they appeared to enjoy swimming around in dirty muddy water like that which filled the paddy fields in the valleys, they could not abide a fresh water stream.

Originally it had not been expected that the parachutist groups would remain in Karenni during the monsoon. But when it became evident that the battle was likely to continue for a while in that area, it was felt that the local villagers could not be left unsupported, and we were told that we should not be withdrawn until November. Both Jerry and I were at that time due for repatriation, and one of the original attractions of the operation had been that it was expected to be a short one. So this news depressed us.

All this time Jerry had been working up at the main headquarters on Mount Plakho where he had been staff officer to Colonel Howell. When Howell returned from Rangoon, Jerry came over to stay with me for a few days. I had just moved into a little jungle camp on the hillside near the Christian village. Such places are built very quickly in Karenni, and I felt much happier at being a little off any beaten track. The morning that Jerry arrived a Lysander was due to land, and it came in while we were busy eating our early morning meal bringing a tall fair haired young Scots corporal called Storrie, who had worked as a wireless operator with the Partisans in Yugoslavia. Castledine, the Flight Sergeant pilot, came up to the new camp and drank a cup of tea while the stores that were in the aeroplane were being unloaded. Then we all walked down with him to the strip and he attempted to start the engine. It showed no signs of life. Castledine tinkered for a little, and then announced that the battery was flat and that he would have to spend the night at my camp. We went back up the hill to drink more tea and draft a wireless message to Rangoon to explain what had occurred.

That morning I had sent off a section of mobile levies down the track leading south to a little village called Simudo, which was at the foot of a pass on the way to a village that the Karens called Mithebu in the foothills above the Sittang. While we were drinking our tea two bursts of automatic fire sounded from that direction. For a moment I took the automatic fire to be from friendly weapons, but then I suddenly remembered that I had not sent a Bren gun with the Simudo party.

Quickly Jerry and I paraded the Gurkhas and Karens in camp and hurried down to the air strip with every automatic weapon that we could lay our hands on. As we reached the foot of the hill I saw the mobile levies from the Simudo track appear at the other side of the paddy and come running across towards us. One of them had been grazed by a bullet just above his left eye and was bleeding hard. Another was apparently missing.

The section commander, a great big hulking fellow who had been in the police before the Japanese invasion, reported that they had walked into a party of Japanese on the track and that there had been a brisk encounter during which both sides had fired wildly. When the Japanese had opened up with a Bren gun and a mortar the levies had decided that it was time to be away.

We took up our position in the bed of the *chaung* that ran across the north end of the air strip with two Bren guns and a two inch mortar which Havildar Bom Bahadur put into position on the hill side to the left of us. In front of us there was a stretch of four hundred yards of open paddy with the Lysander standing in the middle almost directly in our line of fire. We were an odd, motley collection lying there in the undergrowth with our heads sticking over the bank of the *chaung* and our eyes glued on the bushes on the other side of the valley.

There were Jerry and Castledine, who had produced a .38 pistol and was looking surprisingly cool and collected for some one experiencing this sort of thing for the first time. Then there was Saw Digay's youngest son, a boy of fourteen who was working for Jerry as a batman in order to improve his knowledge of English. He had a .22 rifle that we used occasionally when shooting for the pot. Beside them Rabe Thapa had brought a Bren gun into position and Corporal Storrie was checking his carbine magazines. I caught his eye as I passed down the line, and he asked in a rather bored voice whether this happened every day. To the left the remainder of the Gurkhas and mobile levies stretched in a long line. The headman and the village school master at this stage appeared with a party of static levies from Lipeykhi village bringing a touch of colour into the picture with their red and white shirts.

I crawled back up the bed of the *chaung* to where Jerry was lying and told him that if and when the enemy appeared on the other side of the air strip I proposed to open fire with all that we had for a few minutes and then withdraw to the other side of the village. Castledine told us that there was only one piece of mechanism on the Lysander that should definitely not fall into Japanese hands, but doubted whether an ordinary party of Japanese infantry would appreciate the significance of it.

Rabe Thapa saw them first. They came out of the jungle where the Simudo track ran off to the south and the leading section halted as they saw the aeroplane. For a few seconds they were in a bunch at four hundred yards range and I gave Rabe Thapa the order to open fire. There was little chance of inflicting casualties at that distance, but it seemed more important to me to bluff them into believing the air strip was strongly held in the hope that they would withdraw.

The magazine on the Bren gun was loaded with tracer and I saw quite clearly that Rabe Thapa's initial burst did not go very wide of its mark. The Japanese disappeared into the jungle like greased lightning, and then we all opened up with every weapon available. Our fire cannot have been very effective, but as a firework display it was magnificent. Rifles, Stens and Bren guns were chattering away merrily and one of the statics was even firing a Japanese revolver. From the hill side Havildar Bom Bahadur Gurung's two inch mortar brought a heavier note into the proceedings. As I glanced down the line I even saw an original Tower musket being brought onto the scene. This was certainly not a weapon that we had issued to the Karens and it must have been a relic from one of the early Burmese wars when we had probably been fighting our present allies.

I waited for about four minutes and then blew two long blasts on my whistle. This was the pre-arranged signal to withdraw. I crossed the stream at the foot of the little hill on which our jungle camp stood and clambered up the slope through the bamboos with the village headman and a Gurkha and Saw Digay's little son. When I reached the camp I found most of the mobiles and half the Gurkhas assembled there, but there was no sign of Jerry, Casteledine or Storrie. Down at the foot of the hill the fire had ceased and a dead silence had closed over the valley.

We waited a quarter of an hour and then I decided that Jerry must have withdrawn in another direction, and we moved to another position above the Lipeykhi animist village. There we waited about an hour until a Karen arrived with a message from the village schoolmaster written in very quaint English containing the news that the Japanese had withdrawn and that Jerry was down in the village. He had stayed behind when we withdrew and sent out scouts a little later to discover the lie of the land. From the start of the battle he had been considerably more optimistic about its outcome than I had and this had been justified by events.

We slept in a paddy hut by the animist village, and sent out scouts again at dawn. These returned about an hour later to report that the air strip was entirely clear of enemy and that the Lysander was undamaged except for a single bullet mark on its fuselage which we later found to be at a very unimportant place.

During the morning the Flight Lieutenant, Peter Arkell, came in with a fitter and a new battery, which we had bespoken in a wireless message sent off by hand to Mount Plakho the previous evening, and Castledine's aeroplane was soon in a state to depart. The surface of the landing strip had deteriorated a good deal since a Lysander had last taken off from it and although it was still suitable for landing on, it was a little too muddy to enable an aeroplane that was taking off to gather sufficient speed.

My heart came into my mouth as I saw Peter Arkell's Lysander moving up the second half of the strip without its wheels leaving the ground. He only just cleared the bushes by the *chaung* at the north end. Castledine's aeroplane was less heavily loaded and his take-off was not so frightening to watch. But I was not surprised when we received a wireless message from Mount Plakho the following day telling us that Peter Arkell had declared the strip to be no longer suitable until the end of the monsoon.

Jerry was very anxious to discover an all weather air strip that we could keep going throughout the monsoon. I was convinced that this was quite impossible, and adopted a very pessimistic attitude whenever he raised the matter. But he persisted in his search and one day returned to camp with the news that he had at last located a suitable place. I walked over with him to view it the following morning. It was at the far end of the valley that ran south from the Lipeykhi animist village and consisted of a stretch of grass on a hard rock surface from which the rain drained into a nearby stream. There was a paddy hut standing at the end from which the Lysanders would have to come in to land, but Jerry announced that we should have to take it down. On the other side of the hut there was an uphill slope for about three hundred and fifty yards running into the prevailing winds, and Jerry decided that it was a practical proposition. I took a look at a large bump in the ground in the middle of the proposed strip and pooh-poohed the whole idea. But Jerry was quite insistent, and that evening sent for the headman and issued instructions for the paddy hut to be taken down.

A few days later it was arranged that an RAF officer should come over to reconnoitre and report on its suitability. I remained very sceptical, but Jerry's persistence was rewarded when Peter Arkell arrived early one morning in a Lysander and without receiving any signal from the ground came in and made a perfect landing. Apparently the strip looked better when viewed from the air than it did from the ground, and Peter Arkell told me afterwards that when he clambered out of his aeroplane and took a walk around he gasped at his own audacity. Having, however, once landed on it, he was not in a position to declare it impossible. The air strip was a geographical fluke that stood us in very good stead throughout the monsoon. But the pilots hated it and with good reason because it left no margin for error.

A few days later Colonel Howell sent Jerry a message recalling him to main headquarters. A big Japanese withdrawal was taking place down the main track running east of the Yunzalin through Kawludo to Papun, and both Wilson and Bachit were having their areas overrun with Japanese. After Jerry went my main pre-occupation was rations. The Lipeykhi area was by that time practically without rice, and although I had arranged with Colonel Howell for a rice drop, the villagers were very worried. The monsoon had by that time set in in earnest and each day the mountain tops were swathed in mist. I began to doubt whether a Dakota or a Liberator would ever be able to find its way up the valleys.

Just when I had decided that it would never come and was wondering how the levies were going to be fed during the monsoon, the promised rice sortie was delivered. A number of the bags which were dropped free without parachutes fell into the stream running along the valley, but a vast multitude of villagers of all ages and sexes from every village within miles appeared upon the scene miraculously with baskets and elephants and practically everything was safely salvaged. I learnt that even the rice that had been retrieved from the water was edible as long as it was consumed without delay, and we accordingly issued it to the neighbouring villages to be eaten the following day.

The faces of all the Karens took on a more cheerful expression as soon as they saw the rice and realized that the danger of famine was averted. Up till then they had been fighting for the Allies because of an old loyalty that they remembered from before the coming of the Japanese, but after the arrival of the rice they realised for the first time that we were really in a position to help them. We built some jungle caches for the rice in places on the mountain where it seemed unlikely that the Japanese would go even if they were to occupy the Lipeykhi area in force. Then we arranged booby traps with hand grenades in all the caches and detailed a party of static levies whose duty it would be to connect up the booby traps on receipt of news that a large body of enemy was approaching.

At this time reports began to come in from the villages on the other side of the mountains in the direction of Mithebu that there was a large body of Japanese in the Kyaukkyi area. As our information was that Shwegyin was occupied by our own troops, it seemed likely that the enemy would be passing through our area shortly en route for Siam. I had never been very happy about the tactical aspects of our position, situated as we were in a valley, but the protection and operation of the landing strip had become our major commitment, and we had so far inspired the local Lipeykhi villagers to resist the enemy that it seemed impossible to leave them to their fate at that stage. I did however send Rabe Thapa off with a party to a remote little village called Timukhi on the mountain to the north-east to establish a store base and wireless station.

As soon as it was ready Jerry sent me over the Burma Signals operator called Hau Chin Lian who had been helping out the operators at main headquarters.

From time to time small parties of Japanese stragglers would pass through the area in an easterly direction. Before the onset of the rains they had all tended to head south towards Papun once they had crossed the mountains from the Sittang valley. But this route ran down a very narrow defile on the southern side of the Thelaw Klo which was known as the Bilin Chaung. In the dry weather this was little more than ankle deep and it was possible to wade along the bed. But now it was reported to be a surging torrent and the route to the south was practically impassable.

Accordingly the general line of withdrawal seemed to be in a north easterly direction towards Lomati, where it was possible to cross the swollen Yunzalin Chaung on bamboo rafts, and thence down the east bank through Kawludo to Papun. But although there were many rumours of a large Japanese force approaching from Mithebu, the parties that we encountered were small and in poor heart and the static levies were generally successful in chasing them off the main tracks. During that period one Japanese per day was being killed on an average in my sub-area. Each morning pathetic little collections of photographs, identity discs, picture postcards and bone seals were brought in for me to inspect.

Both the Gurkhas and I were by this time feeling the strain. Although we had sufficient rice, there was very little else with which to vary our diet. To begin with we had been able to purchase a certain amount of fresh meat from the local villagers, but their supplies were by this time getting short. Bamboo shoots and various types of edible root that the Gurkhas and Karens knew about were a fairly palatable substitute for fresh vegetables.

I sometimes felt that there were far too many men with only European experience at the supply end of the organisation. Excellent though they may have been in devising suitable ration scales for the French or Greek resistance movements, they were totally unaware of the requirements of Gurkhas. I repeatedly asked for the ordinary Army field scale ration, to be supplied, but it was never sent. This would have included *dhal*, a kind of lentil without which the Gurkhas consider that their meals are un-appetising. As it was the store was full of tins of bully beef which their religion forbade them from eating.

One morning there was the sound of rifle fire from the village of Bikodo in the mountains to the west, and later in the day a boy was brought in with a bullet wound in his buttock. A party of Japanese stragglers had appeared out of the jungle when he was ploughing a field, and had shot him down without more ado. He had bled a good deal before he came to me, and was in a very weak condition. His wound stank horribly and I suspected that gangrene was developing. I poured sulfanilimide powder into the wound, and asked main headquarters to bespeak a Lysander to evacuate him to hospital. As it happened the weather was particularly bad during the next few days, and none of the pilots succeeded in finding the valley. In the meantime De Wanjea, the doctor, came over from headquarters and attempted an operation, but there was no apparatus with us for giving a blood transfusion, and the boy died from shock the following night.

After the doctor returned to main headquarters the rumours that the Japanese force in the Mithebu area would move in our direction became more general. But I had by this time ceased to take them very seriously. From the Tibawkhi villagers to the north-east I learned that there was a party of seven or more Japanese stragglers camping in a ravine on the mountain behind us, and each day shots were exchanged between them and our levies. Finally after they had remained in the ravine for five whole days I sent up Havildar Bom Bahadur with the two inch mortar to see whether a few HE bombs might hasten them on their way.

After he had gone I went down to the *chaung* by the original landing strip to have a bath. I stripped down to a pair of underpants which I invariably retained out of respect for the feelings of the Gurkhas and Karens, soaped myself all over and then lay on my back in the shallow water and allowed the current to wash the lather away. I was aroused by Saw Bla Baw with the news that a large body of Japanese was approaching up the track from Simudo.

I donned my clothes as quickly as possible, trying at the same time not to appear in any way rushed. By the time that I was ready Man Bahadur had appeared on the scene with a Bren gun and a dozen levies. We bemoaned the fact that on this day of all days the Havildar should be away with the mortar, which was by far the most sophisticated weapon that we possessed. But in its absence we decided to do the best we could with a new form of grenade discharger that threw a bomb as far as three hundred yards with fair accuracy. It was too late to move forward onto the Simudo track to lay an ambush, so we took up exactly the same position as in the previous battle when the Lysander had been immobilised on the landing strip.

About a quarter of an hour later Man Bahadur saw three Japanese appear out of the jungle about three to four hundred yards away. They peered carefully across in our direction, but without the slightest hope of seeing us. Then they were joined by several more and the party adjourned to the paddy hut nearby. I screwed a discharger onto the end of a rifle, put a ballastite round into the breach and primed a bomb. My eyesight is not particularly good, but Man Bahadur reported that the Japanese had found a bag of rice that had been left behind by the villagers working in the fields earlier in the morning and were sitting around it in the hut. I cocked up the rifle to an angle of forty-five degrees in the direction of the hut and fired. The bomb burst within fifty feet of it and the enemy dived helter skelter through a hole in the wall and scattered into the jungle. Man Bahadur gave them two bursts from the Bren gun to speed them on their way.

After that I gave the order to cease fire, and we lay quietly in the undergrowth with our eyes glued on the opposite end of the air strip for about half an hour. There was no sign of movement. Finally I decided that it was not wise to remain any longer in the position from which we had originally opened fire even if the enemy had apparently withdrawn. So we crawled back along the bed of the *chaung* in the direction of the small ridge that separated the old and new landing strips and took up a position in the bamboos overlooking the whole valley. From there the Gurkhas reported that there was a large party of Japanese moving about in the jungle along the Simudo track. We picked out a column of smoke rising from the trees and a sentry crouching in the bushes slightly to the east of the position in which they were bivouacing. By this time the headman of Lipeykhi had arrived with the schoolmaster and the Home Guard and we took up positions astride all the little tracks running across the low ridge running north and south. I still believed that the enemy would probably move south-east after they had finished their meal.

Late in the afternoon Havildar Bom Bahadur returned with the two inch mortar, having heard of the arrival of the Japanese. Shortly afterwards a light drizzle of rain started to fall and this later developed into a steady tropical downpour. I suppose that the Japanese must have decided that whoever had fired on their leading elements must have lost interest and withdrawn by this time. Just as darkness was falling we picked out large bodies of men moving about on the old landing strip. Man Bahadur told me that he could see distinctly a very fat Japanese officer regarding with curiosity the hut where we had lived for a time when we first arrived in Lipeykhi and by which we had erected a long bamboo pole for the Colonel's wireless aerial on the night when he passed through.

The Japanese were accompanied by about fifty or sixty Burmese men and women who had obviously been impressed in the plains as coolies. This was a new feature in my sub area and suggested that this was by far the most important party that we had encountered to date. Earlier in the day I had sent Rabe Thapa with a Bren gun team down into the area of the new landing strip in case enemy patrols should be pushed across the little ridge further to the south. Just as night fell heavy LMG fire opened from that direction.

I withdrew my men up to the little camp that we had built on top of the ridge and held a council of war. We had surrounded it with a high stockade of timber and a belt of short bamboo stakes with sharpened ends protruding out of the ground. We could doubtless have made a stiff fight of it in that position, but I did not consider it was our role to engage the enemy in positional warfare. Man Bahadur was all for fighting it out to the last round and the last man, but Bom Bahadur took my view that to us scope for manoeuvre was essential.

In the end I decided to withdraw to Balawkhi and operate from there the following day. Man Bahadur was extremely disappointed at this decision, and I suspect that he purposely decided to disobey my orders. Be that as it may, he succeeded in detaching himself from our party as we scrambled through the jungle in the darkness and when we reached Balawkhi it was reported that he was absent with two other Gurkhas and the two inch mortar.

It was pitch dark when we arrived in the village and we were soaked to the skin. But we received a most cordial welcome from the Karens and ate a great meal of pork and rice washed down with bottles of rice spirit. I felt a little depressed at not having been able to frighten the Japanese out of the Lipeykhi area and wondered whether I should really have stayed and fought it out to the end in my old camp. It was the old problem that faces all guerilla officers sooner or later and which I had experienced before with the Naga hillmen east of Imphal. The big chiefs order you into an area to organise the local population's resistance. You win their confidence and for a while it is all very easy because the Japanese are not expecting to be attacked or ambushed in country which they regard as being under their control. Then after the initial surprise they move in large bodies of regular troops and start to take reprisals against the villagers for having helped you in the first place. You are powerless to do much to hinder the Japanese and indeed have fulfilled the orders that you have received from your own superiors and are at liberty to withdraw. But you have let down the villagers who have helped you in the first place. They come to you beseeching you to send for help to fight the Japanese, but you know that the powers that be will never agree to deploy large bodies of regular infantry just because a few guerillas have fallen into difficulties up in the mountains. I suppose that a great guerilla faced with such a situation would sacrifice himself in one last great battle in the country where he started his revolt, and not hope to escape with his life. But I am not of the stuff of which martyrs are made. Man Bahadur was perhaps more in the epic tradition than I shall ever be. That night, after losing himself in the darkness, he slept in an empty paddy hut not two hundred yards from those where the Japanese were camping. At dawn he placed the two inch mortar in position on the little ridge overlooking the paddy field with a Bren gun beside it and opened fire. The Japanese were taken completely unawares and a good many of the Burmese coolies took the opportunity to bolt into the jungle. When order was restored, the Japanese commander having evidently decided that the area was unhealthy, formed up his men, who Man Bahadur estimated to number not less than 350, and moved north.

My party had taken up positions astride all the tracks leading north-east in the direction of Balawkhi and Tibawkhi. The latter village had a very flourishing home guard organisation led by an ex-armed policeman who had been one of Seagrim's stalwarts, and he had brought over his entire force to reinforce us during the night. I expected the enemy to move due east to Pyagawpu or in our direction as their objective was fairly obviously Siam. But just to reassure Padre Saw Pathaw at Hikholawdo I had sent him a Bren gun to stiffen up his organisation. Much to my surprise I learned later in the day that the Japanese, after leaving Lipeykhi without occupying the village, had proceeded due north to Hikholawdo.

*

By nightfall I was back in Lipeykhi where I found the indomitable Man Bahadur drinking a bottle of rice spirit in the animist village. He was in very good heart and had obviously become something of a hero to the Karen villagers for the way in which he had harassed the Japanese during the morning. Two of Saw Pathaw's scouts came in later with the rather garbled report that a great battle had been fought between the levies and the enemy in Hikholawdo.

Then a Shan prisoner was brought in. He had accompanied the Japanese from the Sittang valley and had taken the opportunity to escape when Man Bahadur had opened fire in the morning. I interrogated him with the aid of Saw Bla Baw who spoke Burmese as well as English and Karen. The Japanese, the Shan said, had originally numbered about six hundred and had light machine guns and mortars. It was rather difficult to follow on the map their route from the account of it that he gave, as most of the villages in the plains had a Karen name as well as a Burmese one and very often a Shan one as well, and more often than not the name by which he referred to a particular village was not the name by which it was marked on the map. But the party appeared to have come from the Pegu Yomas and crossed to the east bank of the Sittang somewhere south of Toungoo about fifteen days before. Thence they had moved south to Kyaukkyi which was apparently empty except for a few odd military policemen and Burmese puppet forces working for the Japanese. They had spent a few days in Kyaukkyi where rice had been collected from the neighbouring villages and a force of coolies conscripted. Then they had moved up into the hills and foraged for a while in the area of Khedo, which the Karens referred to as Mithebu and which I was unable to identify on the map until one very old man came forward with the information that a long time before the village had had another name.

The Shan told us that at Mithebu the Japanese had split up into two parties, and that he had come on with the first party numbering about 350 leaving the ramainder behind. He said that the Japanese had no maps and that there were many sick hobbling along as best they could in the party. One of the Japs had apparently spoken very good Burmese and been able to ask the locals in the plains about routes through mountains. But up in the hills they had found the villages empty wherever they went, and had been hopelessly lost for days.

The villagers apparently accepted the Shan as a victim of the Japanese rather than as a collaborationist, and showed no desire to kill him. I told the headman to give him a place to sleep in the village, but to watch him carefully until the enemy party had moved on from Hikholawdo.

We slept that night in a paddy hut close to the animist village, and in the morning I sent scouts out to Hikholawdo to try and bring back news of Saw Pathaw. They came back in the evening with the ex-armed policeman from Tibawkhi. He had sniped at the Japanese with a Bren gun early that morning from the hillside above the village and been chased a considerable distance by enemy patrols. The Japanese were still in the village. Apparently Saw Pathaw had ambushed them on the track from Lipeykhi and then withdrawn into the hills to the north in the direction of a village called Tichikhi. All the villagers begged me to send a wireless message to headquarters asking for an air strike on Hikholawdo, and I could not make them understand that it was quite impossible for a fast fighter aeroplane to find the village with the clouds as low as they were on the mountains.

The following day I organised an ambush on the track from Simudo in case the remainder of the Japanese party should be following close on the heels of the first. Scouts from the Hikholawdo area reported that the Japanese had slaughtered the livestock and set fire to the houses and moved on into the paddy fields north of the village. There was still no news of Saw Pathaw and the enemy seemed to separate his men from mine.

The next day the enemy did at last move north-east towards the Yunzalin Chaung and the atmosphere became a little less tense. But the respite was only a short one, for shortly after dawn the following day, when I was sitting with my feet dangling over the edge of the hut drinking an early morning cup of tea, the old headman Saw Japo rushed into the camp rolling his eyes, and gesticulating in the direction of Tibawkhi. After spending a night in the jungle the Japanese now appeared to be heading south-east. They had burned Blogawdo after looting what rice caches they could find in the jungle and that very day their advanced elements

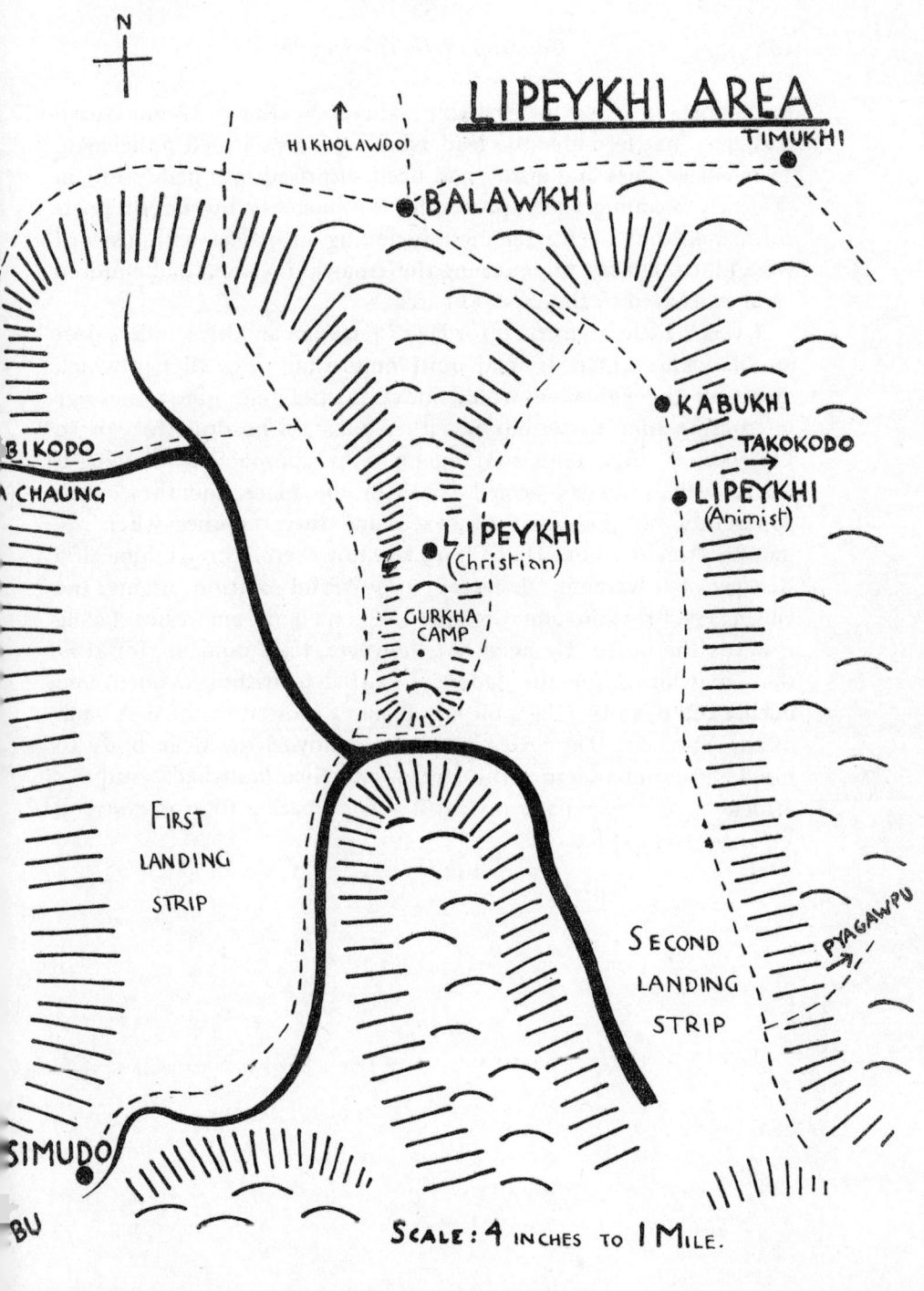

LIPEYKHI AREA

N

↑ HIKHOLAWDOI

TIMUKHI

● BALAWKHI

BIKODO

CHAUNG

● KABUKHI

→ TAKOKODO

● LIPEYKHI
(Animist)

LIPEYKHI
(Christian)

GURKHA
CAMP

FIRST
LANDING
STRIP

SECOND
LANDING
STRIP

→ PYAGAWPU

SIMUDO

BU

SCALE: 4 INCHES TO 1 MILE.

had appeared close to Tibawkhi. There the Karen Home Guard had given battle under the leadership of the ex-armed policeman. Two village girls and a boy had been surprised in a paddy hut in the early morning and captured by the Japanese, but later reports confirmed that twelve Japanese including an officer with a sword were killed. During the morning the Tibawkhi women and children were evacuated to the Lipeykhi area.

I was a little concerned for Hau Chin Lian and his wireless post at Tibawkhi, and it seemed quite impossible to predict in which direction the Japanese would move next. I sent him a message instructing him to withdraw either to main headquarters or to Lipeykhi if large bodies of enemy ever approached his village. There were only six armed levies in the place and these were apparently on the point of evacuating their families when my message reached him. Hau Chin Lian, however, although himself a stranger to Karenni, delivered a powerful oration urging the villagers to remain and organised a screen of ambushes facing towards the north. He need not, however, have done so, for after the Tibawkhi battle the Japanese started to withdraw north and during the next two days the whole party crossed to the east bank of the Yunzalin. The levies in the area allowed the main body to build rafts and to cross the stream and then launched a surprise attack on the rearguard just as it was preparing to cross. Several Japanese were killed.

5

Each time this last large body of Japanese had moved it had left
behind small parties of sick and stragglers too tired to keep pace
with the main column. During the next few days these elements
began to appear in our area, and very few of them escaped to tell
the tale. Mindful of the Shan's report that a strong rearguard was
following behind, we approached them with great care. But for the
most part they avoided the main tracks and attempted to find
their way north-east along the game paths that lay like a network
across the whole countryside.

Jerry sent me a message from Mount Plakho that both Turrall
and Neville reported that there were now practically no Japanese
left along the east bank of the Sittang and that contacts had been
established with the regular troops operating on the west bank
along the tarmac road and railway running south to Rangoon from
Mandalay. The Japanese that had escaped from western Burma
and from the Arakan were still collecting in the Pegu Yomas and
showed no signs to date of attempting a break-out across the
Sittang River in the direction of Moulmein and Siam. On the
Mawchi road the regular troops were held up at about the
twenty-second milestone where a bridge had been blown by the
Japanese across what was a swirling torrent in the monsoon. It
seemed unlikely that much further progress would be made in that
area until either the enemy withdrew of their own accord or the
dry weather came.

Then one morning representatives from the Home Guard in
Simudo came in to report that a small party of Japanese had
appeared on the outskirts of their village at dawn and been driven
off after a brief encounter. Thinking that this was just another
party of stragglers, I thanked them for the information and sent
them back with a little further ammunition. Later in the day
however the whole village evacuated into the Lipeykhi area and I
learnt that there were 'plenty Japs' coming from the east.

Next morning we accordingly moved out with our entire force of mobile levies reinforced by as many of the Home Guard as could be spared from their work in the paddy fields and took up ambush positions facing in the direction of Simudo. At about ten o'clock I received a message from the new landing strip that Jerry had himself arrived and, rather puzzled, I went back to meet him. I found him in a little hut on the edge of the field where the party manning the air field for the day brewed cups of tea and which we referred to as the 'Pilots' Restaurant'. Jerry had received a wireless message the previous night recalling him to Rangoon, where he was apparently required at V Force headquarters. I had expected this summons to come sooner or later as Jerry was far too big a man to be kept sitting around at Plakho as a staff officer to someone else. But I was sorry to hear that he was going. There were very few Britishers on the ground in Karenni, and each one of them was somehow very important.

Colonel Howell had apparently crossed the Yunzalin in the direction of Bachit's sub-area a few days before and was out of wireless contact with us. Jerry had sent off runners to recall him to Mount Plakho, but doubted whether they would find him for several days. In the meantime he felt it essential that an officer should replace him temporarily at main headquarters. Knowing my antipathy to office work he was somewhat reluctant to detail me, but there was no one else available. I said that I would go over the following day, and shortly afterwards the aeroplane arrived. There were some letters for me from home and some copies of the Army newspaper *Seac*. I told Jerry to use all his influence to see that my repatriation was not delayed longer than was absolutely necessary.

No Japanese came north that day from Simudo and I decided that the reports of the villagers must have been exaggerated. I read my mail through a good many times and allowed myself to feel thoroughly homesick. Outside it was raining very hard and the sound of the raindrops beating against the roof of my hut went to increase my melancholy. At dawn I drank a cup of tea and set forth for Mount Plakho.

I had not made the journey since the onset of the monsoon and this time it was very different from before. One could no longer look back from time to time as one marched and see the Lipeykhi valley with its neat rows of paddy fields extending below one like a jig-saw puzzle. Instead one climbed steadily into a strange world in which the trees and bushes were deformed by mist, and all the while the rain fell continuously, leaving one very little inclination to halt and rest beside the track.

I had as an escort two of the mobile levies from the Mount Plakho area who had come over with Jerry the previous day. Both were boys in their middle teens and I decided that they were not as soldierly as the ones that I had trained with the Gurkhas at Lipeykhi. At main headquarters the mobile levies led a very easy existence. We stopped for breakfast at Takokodo and ate a fine steaming pork curry and washed it down with bottles of rice beer which left me in such a deliciously sleepy condition that I felt most loth to embark on the last stage of our journey up onto Mount Plakho. The headman told me that there had been firing from the direction of Pyagawpu the previous day, and I decided that the Japanese party must have moved due east from Simudo instead of passing through Lipeykhi. Little did I know but at that very time they were approaching Takokodo, and on my way to main headquarters I cannot have missed them by more than an hour.

Mount Plakho rises to very nearly 6,000 feet, and is unique in that in the monsoon season, when most of Karenni's jungles are infested with leeches, there are very few on its slopes. To the Karens it is by way of being a holy mountain and there is a legend dating back to the mythical days of the early wars between the Shans and the Karens that at one time a beautiful Karen princess took refuge there and that at the time of her capture by the Shans a prophecy was made to the effect that if ever Karenni was invaded, salvation would come from Mount Plakho and Pyagawpu. Be that as it may Guthrie had been taken there after breaking his leg in his parachute jump, and it had finally been chosen as the site of main headquarters for Hyena Area.

This was in a jungle camp above the village of Chawida and well away from the beaten track. It would have been a magnificent position for a dry weather camp, for it was well above the altitude at which one encounters mosquitos and from it one had a splendid view across the whole valley. But in the rainy season the whole area was perpetually swathed in a blanket of mist that never lifted from week's end to week's end. At night the air was very damp and every morning one found that one's belongings were covered with an evil-looking grey mildew. The Karen levies regarded it as the height of stupidity to live in such an outlandish place during the monsoon. That is a season when oriental peoples make themselves comfortable around the fire places in their own houses, never sallying forth unless it is really necessary, and they regard the Britisher's efforts to maintain business as usual at such times as pure masochism.

At the time when I took over from Jerry at Mount Plakho there were three British NCO wireless operators at main headquarters. In addition to the Sergeant Moore who had hidden with Duncan Guthrie on the mountain in the very early days of the operation, there was the Scots Corporal Storrie who had been in Yugoslavia and the minute Sergeant Rowe who had grown a big black beard in Karenni. Rowe had started life with the intention of becoming a Roman Catholic priest, but he had apparently found himself in a seminary belonging to a Belgian order whose brand of Catholicism was not congenial to him, and had accordingly reverted to the laity. For a while he had been a salt salesman and at the same time an enthusiastic Territorial. When the war came, he had joined a Commando, and from there he was chosen to go into the French *maquis* on account of his facility with the French language acquired during his period in the seminary.

The Colonel had trained a group of the better educated Karens for code work. This department was controlled by Padu. He was a very well educated man and his command of the English language was exceptional. He would even from time to time introduce a sophisticated little gallicism into his conversation, although he had no real knowledge of French as such. But being no longer very young he was not the ideal operational interpreter, and his position as chief of the codes department was very suitable for him.

The most important of the local Karen leaders was the one armed headman of Chawida, who we all referred to as the *thugyi*. He was a lean ascetic figure and spoke good but rather laboured

Gopal Singh Thapa, Fielding and Man Bahadur Chettri at the Lipeykhi air strip

Man Bahadur Chettri, Gopal Singh Thapa and Peter Arkell with some of the levies and the villagers from Lipeykhi

At Mount Plakho Headquarters: Corporal Storrie, Sergeant Moore, Saw San Sein, myself and the doctor, with (*kneeling*) Sergeant Rowe and Padu

English, and was a very enthusiastic Baptist. His great ambition was to see a Seagrim memorial chapel erected in Pyagawpu.

Second only to the *thugyi* was a very charming and venerable old Karen called Saw San Sen. He was officially a Jemadar in the mobile levies, but he was a little too elderly to go out on active operations and was accordingly used in an administrative capacity at main headquarters. One day he told me his story. When the Japanese invasion had started he had already finished eighteen years service in the police and was very nearly due for a pension. He was at the time stationed in a country police station at Lomati. Being in something of a quandary after the British administration had departed, he had finally made the journey to where Seagrim was rumoured to be. Seagrim had told him that the British would certainly return one day, and that if he continued to help them now, he would eventually be sure to get his pension. And so as an old man, poor Saw San Sen found himself actively participating in a guerilla war. He was rounded up by the Japanese after Seagrim's capture, but he was evidently not considered to be important enough for removal to Rangoon, and had been sent back to his village with a warning.

Saw San Sen lived in a little hut close to mine. In the morning I would see him polishing a pair of spectacles that he must have treasured since the days before the Japanese occupation, and then he would settle down to read the Bible. There were also a few old copies of *The Tatler* that had been dropped one day from an aeroplane, and from time to time he would study them with great interest.

Perhaps the greatest of the Karen guerillas was Seagrim's old wireless operator Saw Thet Wa. He was a tall good-looking young man of little more than twenty-one, but when one looked into his eyes one saw that he was already very old and tired. His father had been the headmaster of a school in the Chin Hills on the other side of Burma, where incidentally Hau Chin Lian had been educated. He had been at school in Rangoon at the time when the Japanese came. After his evacuation to India he had enlisted in the RAF but he had not been with them long, for there cannot have been a great many young and active Karen emigrés in India in those days and he was an obvious choice for a resistance worker in Burma.

With Seagrim he had suffered much before his capture. Afterwards he had attempted to head north on his own towards the Mawchi road, but it had been at the time of the monsoon and there had been Japanese *Kempei Tai* in all the villages and in the end he had been surrounded while sleeping in a hut close to Simudo. To begin with the Japanese had not treated him badly, and the platoon commander that had taken him into Rangoon had even offered him cigarettes and rice spirit. But once he was in the central prison his troubles had started in earnest and he had had his fair share of beatings and periods of starvation diet. After his escape and return to the guerillas Colonel Howell had felt it was impossible to evacuate him to the British areas, as his local knowledge was exceptional. But by the time I moved to main headquarters, he was a very sick man and his nerves were very much on edge.

Lastly there was De Wanjea, the Bengali doctor, who was an ardent Congressman and had been imprisoned by the police for political activity before the war. He had been domiciled in Burma since childhood, and regarded himself as a Burman before he was a Bengali.

It was June 20th when I arrived at main headquarters. In Lipeykhi I had not been very well informed about what was happening in the sub-areas other than my own and in the great wide world outside Karenni. After I had eaten my morning meal therefore, which consisted of an Australian jungle ration, I settled down to go through the files from the various outstations from the very beginning of the operation. Each outstation had been allotted a colour by way of easy reference. Over on the Sittang there was Turrall's unit which was described as Hyena Red. He was then living in a camp in the jungle south of Kyaukkyi which he moved every few days for security reasons. Most of the levies considered that these continuous moves were completely unnecessary, especially in view of the Japanese withdrawal from the river bank. But I could well understand Turrall's attitude. He had been in the operation from the very start and before that he had commanded a deception unit in the second Chindit operation that had gone around trying to create the impression that a handful of men were really a British brigade.

In the jungle one tends to grow more and more careful the longer one is on operations, and I noticed in my own case that I suffered from a tendency that was progressively increasing, to read subtleties into every Japanese move which the European breed of guerilla, who had only seen the Japanese in defeat, considered fantastic. In Turrall's sub-area, moreover, there was a mixed population of Shans, Burmese and Karens, and while it was safe to trust one's life to any of the last-named race, one could not feel so confident of the first two.

North of Turrall there was a sub-area called Hyena Purple which was commanded by an epic figure called Neville. I never met Neville, but we exchanged a great many messages and signals and I came to have a tremendous respect for him. He had originally served in the Greek resistance and had from there graduated to Burma where conditions must have been very different. He had come into the Hyena area without any trained parachutists to give him a start, and he had built up an organisation among the villagers at Tiyo-bawkata in the entrance to the Pada valley which was one of the main routes into the hills from the Sittang. Neville never became unreasonable when one was obliged to send him out messages from headquarters which were inconvenient to him, however hard pressed he might be. And in adversity he was indomitable. The bogus showman occurs in every military organisation, and if one received a message on the lines of '2000 Japs approaching with pack artillery. Am going to try and break them up', one would at least take it with a grain of salt. But in the case of Neville I would have been prepared to take it very seriously indeed, and I would also have been quite convinced that Neville would indeed move in to the attack with everything that he had at his disposal. He had not many trained and reliable guerillas in the Pada Chaung, and I always felt that he was to a much larger extent than anyone else a one-man army. If I had a successful encounter, the success of it was as much due to the Gurkhas as it was to me, but in Hyena Purple it was Neville who sited and fired the Bren guns, and laid and detonated the charges, and all his levies were little more than hangers on.

South of Turrall's area the Sittang river jinked towards the west and the stretch of paddy land between the river bank and the foothills became considerably broader. This area included Burmese as well as Karen villages and parties of the Anti-Fascist Organisation operated in proximity to the Karens. Originally a deputation had come up into the hills to see Colonel Howell shortly after the Japanese reoccupation of Kyaukkyi to ask for arms, and an officer called Barron accompanied by a Karen major of the name of Saw Torry had gone down, travelling in bullock carts by night, to organise resistance. For a while operations in the neighbourhood, which came to be known as Hyena White, had gone well, and then Barron had been wounded by a grenade splinter in the foot in a close quarter encounter with the enemy, and had had to be evacuated across the Sittang to the regular troops on the railway line. His British sergeant wireless operator had been evacuated with fever shortly afterwards and Saw Torry had lost wireless contact with main headquarters.

My sub-area in the centre of the mountains was known as Hyena Cerise, a colour association that caused most people who knew me a good deal of amusement. East of the Yunzalin the country descending to the bank of the Salween, which was very wild and sparsely populated, was divided into northern and southern sub-areas known as Orange and Green respectively. Wilson commanded Orange and had with him the French Canadian officer called Fournier. Green was run by Bachit, an elderly Karen major who had been a schoolmaster in Toungoo before the war. At the time when I went to Mount Plakho Colonel Howell was with Bachit, and in view of the difficulty in crossing the Yunzalin Chaung in the monsoon and avoiding the large numbers of Japanese retreating down the main track from Mawchi to Papun which ran beside it it seemed unlikely that he would return for some time. I sent him off a message informing him that Jerry had been recalled and asking him to return, but I was not very optimistic about his ability to do so.

That evening before supper the one-armed *thugyi* came in to see me in the office hut in which I slept and told me that there were large numbers of Japanese all the way along the valley from Pyagawpu to Takokodo. I had heard a few isolated shots fired during the afternoon, but had been so engrossed in absorbing the big picture of the tactical situation that I had ignored them. There seemed, however, nothing that we could do at that stage, and after detailing a section of mobile levies to go out under a rather useless ex-Havildar in the Burma Rifles the following morning and snipe at them from the hillside with a Bren gun, I had my supper and went to bed.

As I lay and listened to the rain beating monotonously against the roof of my hut, I thought of Hau Chin Lian with his little wireless post on top of the hill at Timukhi and wondered what I could do to help him. Before leaving Lipeykhi I had sent him over a Bren gun with Gopal Singh Thapa and Jamkholem Kuki, who were two of the best men that I had, but I began to hope to hell that they would not indulge in any costly heroics against a vastly superior enemy force. Thinking it over I decided that the Japanese were unlikely to make the steep climb up the mountain to Timukhi the next day, and would probably take the easier route north east to the Yunzalin which ran along a valley beside a tributary chaung. Actually I was wrong in the way that one nearly always was in Karenni when one tried to guess which way an enemy party would make its next move.

While we were having breakfast the sound of light automatic fire came floating up from the hillside on the other side of the valley. A few minutes later the explosions of grenades were heard. At the time Sergeant Rowe was on the set. He was a meticulous operator, as indeed he had to be in that kind of work, and he came running over to the office hut practically green in the face. Hau Chin Lian had ignored the code and sent over a message in clear to the effect that his post was being attacked. I found it difficult not to sympathise with Hau Chin Lian in the circumstances and felt that I should have found it impossible myself to have settled down to encode a message with a battle raging around me. But I pacified Sergeant Rowe by agreeing with him entirely and telling him that disciplinary action would have to be taken against Hau Chin Lian later.

By this time the fire had died down in the valley. About an hour later scouts crept down the hill through the jungle, but when they came back at dusk their information was that there were still many Japanese troops in Takokodo. After his fierce rebuke from Sergeant Rowe Hau Chin Lian had gone off the air entirely and might have been dead for all I knew. There being no way in which I could contact either him or Havildar Bom Bahadur at Lipeykhi, I spent an uneasy night. Fortunately it was not a moon period and I knew full well that it was therefore impossible for any of the enemy to make their way up the hillside in the direction of main headquarters after dark. The ex-Burma Rifles Havildar's party had never got in a shot at the Japanese party and I was rather annoyed with him. Apparently the enemy had moved out of Takokodo early in the morning in the direction of Timukhi and returned on their tracks after the battle on the hillside.

Later I learned the full story. The previous evening Hau Chin Lian with Gopal Singh Thapa and Jamkholem Kuki and two Gurkhas with fever that I had sent up to Timukhi to recuperate had learned that the Japanese from Pyagawpu had occupied Takokodo. The Takokodo villagers had withdrawn in some disorder after firing a few shots and spent the night in Timukhi after evacuating their women and children further north in the direction of Tibawkhi. Local morale had been low at the time as a result of the depredations of the last big enemy party, and the levies had wanted to withdraw from the Timukhi area without giving battle. The two sick Gurkhas had been inclined to agree with them, but Hau Chin Lian had made an impassioned speech to the assembled company, and in the end informed everyone that whatever else they might like to do he intended to stay in Timukhi the following day and fight it out with whatever came along. Gopal Singh Thapa and Jamkholem Kuki had agreed to do likewise and the headman of Takokodo had prevailed upon the more stout hearted of his men to form an ambush party.

This had taken up position with two Bren guns and two grenade dischargers at dawn on the tracks running up the hillside in the direction of Timukhi and at about nine o'clock the leading Japanese section had walked straight into them. Being on a steep and slippery slope they had had no chance to disappear into the jungle quickly once the ambush was sprung. The leading five men had been riddled with bullets and left on the track in front of the levies, and their comrades had scattered madly down the hillside into the jungle in the direction of Takokodo with the levies' Bren guns and the grenade dischargers hastening them on their way.

The Japanese are normally very meticulous in burying their dead and removing identity discs and anything else from the bodies that might enable a British intelligence officer to identify their unit, but in this case they never recovered the ground where their comrades fell and four Japanese identity discs were brought in to me two days later. With the help of a list of Japanese numerals in my copy of *Notes for forward units on the Japanese Army* and a list of code serial numbers of the Japanese units in Burma which we had at headquarters I was able to identify them as belonging to the Japanese 72nd Independent Mixed Brigade. This is the sort of information that the intelligence staffs of the big formations are always very pleased to get, as collated on an enormous map in conjunction with all the other identifications that have been obtained in other areas it is often possible to detect enemy movements long before they ever develop into anything big.

That night the Japanese licked their wounds in Takokodo and the following morning they limped off down the valley leading east to the Yunzalin leaving eight of their number in the village in an exhausted condition. At midday the levies descended on this rearguard with a swift rush and no Japanese survivors lived to tell the tale.

6

After that a month of perfect peace descended upon the Cerise sub-area, and to the west both Turrall and Neville were able to move down to the east bank of the Sittang River and liaise with the regular troops on the other side. What Japanese there were in the area west of the Salween apart from the rearguards holding the Mawchi—Kemapyu road and the area south of Papun, were assembling in the Pegu Yomas and making little attempt at the moment to cross the railway line. 2 V Ops were operating into the Pegu Yomas from the bases held by the regular troops along the railway line attempting to find out exactly what the Japanese strength in the area was and what route they would take when they eventually tried to break out across the Sittang. But on the main track running south from Loikaw across the Mawchi road and down through Kawludo and Papun there appeared to be a continuous stream of retreating Japanese. Reports indicated that a great many of them were in appallingly bad condition, and indeed it is difficult to imagine what exactly they found to eat on their way, for the villages in the area were by this time picked bare.

Wilson had started off with a few spectacular ambushes along the main track, and then his entire area had been overrun and for a while he had had to go into hiding in the jungle and existed as best he could on bamboo shoots and roots. His mobile levies were naturally very dispirited, and some of them had deserted. Further south Bachit had been less downright in his methods, and without probably inflicting as many casualties as Wilson on the Japanese had more successfully preserved what little rice there was left in the mountain villages intact.

The Colonel had at last reached Green's headquarters and was busy arranging for an air drop. Earlier on it had not been the policy to mine tracks and lay booby-traps as it was considered that the local Karens would suffer as much from such tactics as the Japanese. But the main track running through Orange and Green sub-area was by this time sedulously avoided by the locals, and the Colonel had decided that at this stage the use of mines on a large scale had become inevitable. Unfortunately, he was thwarted in his plans by the weather. Before the monsoon, it had been a difficult enough business to locate supply dropping zones in the network of mountain *chaungs* and valleys that lay along the Salween, and now that the clouds and mist were always low on the hills, it was well-nigh impossible. From main headquarters we were busy relaying a series of angry and sometimes pathetic messages to Rangoon asking for a drop of explosives. But three weeks passed before, after many abortive attempts, a Dakota found its way through, and by that time the stream of retreating Japanese was slowly coming to an end.

I led a melancholy enough existence during those days, reading and drafting messages, keeping situation maps up to date, and drinking innumerable cups of tea. The wireless operators in the camp were recently out from Europe and I began to realise how out of touch I was with England and the life I wanted to lead after nearly four years in the east. There was at that time a great shortage of reading material, and what little there was invariably consisted of very third rate thrillers of the twopenny blood variety. None of us were exactly highbrow in our tastes, but we all longed for something a little more stimulating. The only classic we possessed was a very battered copy of *Wuthering Heights*, which was passed from hand to hand.

By this time the headquarters area was getting short of rice and in order to feed the mobile levies I made an arrangement with Havildar Bom Bahadur Gurung at Lipeykhi to send me over an elephant load of rice from time to time. Nearly every village in the neighbourhood had in peacetime owned a communal elephant which was used to carry the rice down from the cultivated area on the mountain sides. These were burnt clear at the beginning of each planting season and abandoned the following year after one crop had been gathered in. That year the hill fields had for the most part not been cultivated and the elephants were standing idle, so that the villagers were only too willing to hire them to us. It is difficult really to imagine a less mercenary minded eastern people than the Karens. Even the levies seldom troubled to ask for their pay, and in the end one was usually obliged to send for the local headman and insist on paying for work done whenever any of his villagers had been summoned to build further huts or for other minor chores about the camp. I paid the elephant drivers on the basis of an elephant carrying the loads of six coolies. There was one baby elephant that sometimes came over from Lipeykhi with its mother, and that of course only carried a two-man load.

South of the Thelaw Klo in the wild country along the Bilin Chaung that separated us from Mongoose Area there was no British officer operating. When Jerry left there was a suggestion that some one else should be sent to replace him. But I suppose that the powers that be were by this time beginning to lose interest in an operation that would come to an end as soon as the Japanese in the Pegu Yomas either broke out across the Sittang or were liquidated in the process and week after week I waited on in the main headquarters at Mount Plakho.

The Colonel established contact with an English speaking ex-policeman called Saw Tannay on the west bank of the Yunzalin Chaung just north of Papun and I sent him down supplies of arms and ammunition. After the Japanese 72nd Independent Mixed Brigade had gone through, one party of about eighty enemy was reported to be milling around in the area between Saw Tannay and ourselves. They were most of them wearing Karen and Burmese clothes and were apparently in shocking condition. Probably they were without maps or instructions other than to reach Siam, and each day there would be casualties as a result of the static levies harassing activities or from sickness and exhaustion.

Saw Tannay sent me up some identity discs that he had captured from them and they all bore the serial numbers of 49 Divisional Cavalry Regiment. One collection of photographs that accompanied the discs was extremely interesting in that it might well have been exhibited as a sort of pictorial record of the making of a Japanese soldier. The earlier photographs showed him as a round faced and rather cherubic small boy looking much as small boys look the world over. Then there were family groups in which he appeared to take pride of place as an adored eldest son. Afterwards there was a picture of him as a recruit in the Army, in which he still looked a rather decent young fellow. But in the later pictures his face became progressively harder and more typical of what one imagined a Japanese soldier's would be. Until in the end there was a rather arrogant portrait taken in Rangoon showing him as a hardened veteran from whose face all traces of boyish charm and kindliness had been eradicated. I put this collection aside, intending to retain it as a souvenir, but in the next few weeks the mildew destroyed the pictures. Somehow with my repatriation looming as close as it did, I lost all real interest in souvenirs, and I passed most of the stock pieces such as autographed flags and officer's swords onto Sergeant Rowe and Corporal Storrie who were indefatigable collectors.

One day in the early part of July we received a signal that headquarters desired to send a British journalist broadcasting from an American radio station into Karenni and suggested that the Lipeykhi landing strip might be a suitable place for him to visit. From his fastnesses on the opposite bank of the Yunzalin Colonel Howell was not at all enthusiastic about the scheme, but Sergeant Rowe and the Karens seemed very excited at the prospect of being interviewed. I signalled Rangoon to the effect that there was at present no Britisher in Lipeykhi and suggesting that if the journalist still wished to come he might land at Lipeykhi and come on up to Mount Plakho the following day. We were always glad when an aeroplane landed at the air strip as this meant mail and newspapers and also a few small luxuries such as cigarettes and rum. The walk from Lipeykhi to Mount Plakho was to say the least of it very severe, particularly in the monsoon season, but I had pictured the journalist as being at the most in his early thirties, and had decided that it would do him no harm to get an idea of the conditions under which the guerillas really lived.

Much to my mortification, however, when he turned up it transpired that he was nearly old enough to have been my father. He arrived perched on an elephant just before dusk with an escort of mobile levies under the command of the little Gurkha SurabdhauRai, after we had given up hope of his ever coming. Earlier in the day Corporal Storrie had been certain that he had heard through the mist an aeroplane circling on the other side of the mountains in the direction of Lipeykhi, but by five o'clock we had decided that he must have been mistaken. Michael Fielding was a bulky figure of a man of over fifty, who must have lived a fairly sedentary life for a number of years. Even on an elephant he must have suffered agonies on his journey, and indeed he was almost too stiff to move when the time came to descend to earth. But he made no word of complaint, and indeed when he had thawed out for a while by the fire and been given a meal he announced that he was very glad that he had 'done it the hard way'.

Except for Turrall and the Colonel all of the officers were somewhat youthful and for the Karens it was probably a very excellent thing to meet such an imposing figure as Michael Fielding. He had started off his life as a Regular Indian Army Cavalry officer in the last war, but after the Armistice he had found the life restricted. His father had died shortly afterwards and he had come into money. This had given him the opportunity to leave the Army and emigrate to America where he had tried his hand at cattle ranching. From this he had graduated to Hollywood where he had lost his fortune. After that he had been a crime reporter in Chicago. That had been in the tough days and he had known Al Capone. Parts of his life must have been very hard indeed, but he had made good in the end as a news analyst for the Chicago Broadcasting Station. There, as a Britisher, he was not without political importance, and for this reason he had been able to pull the requisite strings enabling him to get admitted to the guerilla area in Karenni.

Actually a better ambassador could not have been chosen. He was, as I have said, a big man with the weight of years upon him and the Karens were very intrigued. For the Britishers it was a break from the monotony of our everyday life to have him with us, and we enjoyed his visit immensely.

That night we received some very dramatic messages from Wilson on the other side of the Yunzalin. His area had been completely overrun with Japanese and he was hiding in the jungle watching them loot his old camp. In the morning De Wanjea and Corporal Storrie took Fielding down to a little range that we had built in an old disused paddy field a little further down the hill and spent a noisy hour throwing grenades and firing various weapons with the levies.

In the afternoon Fielding produced a small coloured flag presented to him before setting forth on his journey by the Adventurers' Club of Chicago. In order to be a member of this club it was necessary to have at one time or another hazarded one's life in some rather dangerous undertaking, and whenever a member embarked on an expedition he was invariably presented with a flag to take with him on his travels. Sometimes, Fielding informed us, the members had not returned to tell the tale, but the flags had always been eventually recovered. We photographed Fielding with the levies and his flag as proof that he had actually visited the guerilla area, but he told us that most of the members of the Adventurers' Club were of a very cynical turn of mind and asked us for a certificate to hand in with the flag when he returned.

The whole idea was, as Fielding admitted, very American, but we entered into it with great gusto and wrote him out an impressive looking document couched in very schoolboy language to the effect that: 'We the undersigned of the Hyena Guerilla Organisation entertained Captain Michael Fielding at Guerilla Headquarters behind the Japanese lines from blank till blank.' Michael Fielding was hugely pleased at this and was obviously going to have a rare social success producing it when he got back to Chicago. We all felt that we would have liked to have been his guests that evening, as it would undoubtedly be a big occasion. After it was prepared we put a mass signature onto it in English, Karen, Burmese and Hindi, and Corporal Storrie inscribed the black spider as symbol of the organisation. It was an orgy of schoolboy dramatics but we all rather enjoyed ourselves. In the morning Fielding left early for Lipeykhi by elephant and we were sorry to see him go.

A few days later a thin nervous young Karen from the plains with a pleasant disarming smile arrived with a message from Saw Torry. Since Barron's sergeant operator had been evacuated early in May we had been out of wireless communications with White sub-area and the runners that we had occasionally been able to send off generally took about fourteen days on the journey there and back. Just before his departure Jerry had sent off two villagers to

Kywethalin, where Saw Torry was last known to have had his headquarters, asking that an English speaking guide should be sent over to escort Sergeant Moore back with a wireless set. This young man had been sent for this purpose. He had been to the local High School before the coming of the Japanese, and his knowledge of English was adequate.

Jerry had hoped that a spare wireless set which he had bespoken from Rangoon for Saw Torry would have been dropped to us before the arrival of the guide, so that Moore would have been able to set off complete with all his stock in trade. This had not arrived and the question that arose was whether it was worth sending off Sergeant Moore without the wireless. I soon learned when I discussed the matter in the mess hut at night with the sergeant operators that there were other things to consider besides the tactical aspects.

Quite naturally all the British operators would have preferred to serve under a British officer and they were obviously in league to produce every possible objection to Sergeant Moore's departure.

I appreciated their very natural desire to have a fellow country man in their vicinity, for in the days when I had been at Lipeykhi with the Gurkhas on my own I had from time to time felt extraordinarily lonely. But the presence of Saw Torry's English speaking guide combined with the fact that for once, as far as we knew, the route to the Sittang was clear of Japanese, made it a quite unique opportunity to get Sergeant Moore on his way. Discipline in a guerilla unit is on a very different basis from discipline anywhere else. All the British NCOs religiously called me 'Sir', but I felt all the time that the situation was too informal for it to be really necessary.

Finally I summoned Sergeant Rowe and pointed out to him that, while I was quite prepared to keep Moore at Mount Plakho if there was any reason connected with the efficiency of the signals for me to do so, if there was not, it was only right that he should go.

I pointed out to Moore that perhaps the presence of a Britisher in White sub-area would make all the difference between success or failure when the break-out across the Sittang started. In the end the operators became resigned to one of their number departing, and Moore went off in a deluge of rain two days later.

It was at about this date that we began to refer to the 'break-out'. Before we had always been so engrossed in the immediate situation around us that we had had little opportunity to think of the 17,000 odd Japanese massing in the Pegu Yomas. But during the month of July, when there were no Japanese in the area and we were for the most part sitting around in our small bamboo huts listening to the noise made by the rain outside, we began to use the phrase more and more. The implications of the break-out as far as we were concerned on the east bank of the Sittang was not pleasant to contemplate. The Japanese in the Pegu Yomas had been living for many months on what they could forage from the villages, and the majority of them would by then be practically crazed with hunger. Even if the regular troops along the tarmac road and railway line between Toungoo and Pegu killed a great many of them as they crossed, it seemed certain that a fair proportion would get away. And their frame of mind once they had crossed to the east bank would probably be very savage.

From day to day the official theories as to when and where the break-out would start varied. For a while it was believed that the enemy would attempt to retake Pegu and hold it for just long enough to get their main forces across the road from the Pegu Yomas. Colour was lent to this theory by reports from V Force and the various Burmese irregular organisations that there was a big Japanese concentration in the jungle west of Pegu. Then one evening we received a situation report that the enemy had recrossed to the west bank of the Sittang in the area of the Mokpalin bridge and was attacking the Gurkha company in Nyaungkashe in great strength. The following day we learned that our troops had been forced to evacuate Nyaungkashe and it looked very much as if a critical situation was developing. But in the meantime a V Force officer in the Pegu Yomas had reported that the concentrations of enemy due west of Pegu were moving north, and the powers that be rightly deduced that the threat to Pegu was only in the nature of a feint.

About this time an enemy operation order was captured in a

skirmish in the foothills west of Pegu and this gave the date of the break-out as the first day of the full moon early in August. The plan was for the Japanese main body to cross the main road somewhere south of Pegu by moonlight, and it was anticipated that the whole force would be across the river by dawn. The Japanese did in fact adhere to this plan fairly rigidly when the time came. But to us it looked absurd, and indeed it did not subsequently prove to be very successful. Trying to put myself in the place of the Japanese commander, I felt that I should have filtered my men across in small parties over a long period, but perhaps of course the Japanese ration situation was at the time so desperate as to necessitate a mass breakout.

While the tension gradually increased along the main road, we had little to do save sit and wait. The Gurkhas in Lipeykhi had had an air drop of ammunition and explosives and various schemes for mining tracks and laying booby traps in villages and paddy stores were laid on in case it should be necessary. I had seen very little of the Gurkhas during the previous few weeks and was not surprised when I received a little note from my young interpreter Saw Bla Baw and another from Hau Chin Lian reporting that there was trouble brewing up in the section of mobile levies stationed at Timukhi. After the battle Lance-Naik Man Bahadur had gone over to take command from Lipeykhi. I suspect that the Havildar Bom Bahadur was glad enough to have an opportunity to detail him for detachment duty.

As I have said before, Man Bahadur was a Chettri and as such considered himself a cut above any one else in the Gurkha Brigade and Karenni as well. He was probably the best natural soldier I had in my organisation, and he had a kind of reckless animal courage that no one else could hope to emulate. Hau Chin Lian and Saw Bla Baw were both in a state of considerable agitation, as Man Bahadur had been striking various Karens, and making himself extremely unpopular. Being a strict Hindu he was unable to eat bully beef, and in the ration tins that we were using at the time there was very little else. He was using his religion as an excuse for eating all the sardines himself. These were regarded as the best item in the rations by the Karens, and a good deal of bad feeling had been caused. I was anxious not to discourage Man Bahadur, for I would rather have had him beside me in a battle than any one else in the area. But at the same time I could well imagine that he was being extremely difficult.

In the end I decided to close down the wireless station at Timukhi. Man Bahadur took his mobile levies back to join the Havildar on the landing strip at Lipeykhi, and Hau Chin Lian and Saw Bla Baw came in to main headquarters. Hau Chin Lian had fallen heavily in love with one of the village girls in Timukhi and announced his intention of marrying her after the war. As both he and his fiancée were ardent Baptists everything seemed to be in order. But I suggested to him that he would do well to consult his father in the Chin Hills first of all.

Saw Bla Baw had decided that he wanted to join the Regular Army and become a parachutist. I told him that once the break-out had taken place there would be little further need for parachutists in Karenni. But he replied that there were also many Karens in Siam and that after the Japanese crossed the Salween perhaps we could all go there.

Saw Thet Wa, Seagrim's former wireless operator, had been suffering from recurrent bouts of malaria for some time. One day the doctor came to me and asked whether it would be possible for him to be evacuated. Saw Thet Wa had always been on the point of being evacuated ever since he had first escaped from the *Kempei Tai* and joined the guerillas, but he was one of those unfortunate people who are too valuable to be easily replaced. I knew that Colonel Howell would be very loth to see him go, but nevertheless sent a message asking permission to send him out to Rangoon. Rather to my surprise the Colonel agreed without a murmur.

So the same night we celebrated with a bottle of rum, and the villagers from Pyagawpu sent up a little black mountain pig for the feast. And the next morning Saw Thet Wa, already starting to look several years younger, set off for the landing strip at Lipeykhi with instructions to board the next plane.

The last schedule on the wireless was at that time at six o'clock in the evening and Padu with his coders used to decipher the messages received on it by torchlight before they broke off for their supper. While this was going on the doctor, Rowe, Storrie and myself would be eating our meal at the other end of the hut. One evening Padu called down to me that the first few groups of the message upon which he was working were addressed to me personally. Somewhat intrigued I gobbled down the last few mouthfuls of the curry that we were having for supper that night and went down to help him. To my delight the remainder of the message ran '*Your repatriation now available. Longmuir arrives by Lysander soonest to relieve you.*' Out of respect for the others' feelings I tried to conceal my pleasure as much as possible, but it was really extremely difficult. After nearly four years in the east the prospect of going home was enough to render me delirious with joy.

The only message that night was a situation report from Otter Area in the north to the effect that 1,500 aggressive well-armed Japs were moving south from the Mawchi—Kemapyu road. As I lay in bed that night I decided that this was a force moving down to cover the break-out. I carefully calculated the time required for them to cover the ground that separated them from us, and reckoned that it would be quite twenty days. By that time I would be evacuated and it would be up to old Jock Longmuir to give them a warm reception. I felt a twinge of conscience that I should be capable of feeling relieved at escaping from my responsibilities in such circumstances, but I had by that time lost most of my enthusiasm for guerilla warfare, and the rapid approach of my final departure from Burma was the most important thing to me in the world. Little did I know then that I was to see the war through in that country to the bitter end.

The next three weeks were among the most agonising that I can remember. Each evening I expected a message from headquarters to the effect that Longmuir would be flown in the following day, and instructing me to go down to the air strip at Lipeykhi to await his arrival. But not a word did I receive. Each day the situation reports pinpointed the Japanese force from the Mawchi road as a stage further south. North-west of Neville's sub area in the plains along the bank of the River Sittang there was an area in which the Anti-Fascist Organisation was operating under an officer called Waller. From him we received a message for onward transfer to

Neville that this force was well armed and equipped and exceptionally aggressive and heading south through the foothills.

I was curious to see what Neville's reaction would be to these terrifying reports. He went out and ambushed the enemy on the south bank of the Mon Chaung to the north of his sub-area and inflicted fairly heavy casualties in the initial encounter. But the following day they moved forward again in a more tactical fashion, crossing the river in many different places. Being out-flanked Neville withdrew to Tiyo-bawkata where he must have spent a feverish night laying a network of primer cord with explosive charges attached all round the villages. In the morning he let the enemy enter the village and then blew the charge. In the ensuing confusion he had to beat a very hasty retreat without ascertaining the extent of the damage caused, but later some sixty bodies were dug up from communal graves in the area. That night, however, even the irrepressible Neville must have been a little depressed. He sent us a rather cynical message to the effect that *'These Japs are bad tempered bastards. It's a good life while it lasts'*.

Two days later the enemy column moved on up the Pada Chaung in the direction of Mithebu, and I decided that they must indeed be a covering force to enable the Japanese troops breaking out of the Pegu Yomas to reach the east bank of the Sittang without opposition. Both Neville and Saw Torry had had ambitious plans for lining the river bank with a string of guerilla posts to shoot up the enemy in mid-stream as they attempted to cross. But as a result of this force's movement all the guerillas had been driven back into the foothills.

But I was proved to be wrong. The Japanese turned east into the hills half way up the Pada Chaung and I began to receive excited messages from my scouts along the track leading into Bikodo to the effect that fantastic numbers of Japanese were approaching. The villagers' capacity for giving an accurate report of the strength of hostile parties was very limited. It was seldom that one could persuade them to go about the business system- atically and sit beside a track all day and count the number of enemy that passed along it. I had come to know from past experience that any force of over three hundred was invariably

reported as ten thousand. Sure enough on this occasion Havildar
Bom Bahadur learned from the villagers that this number was
coming.

I knew that I should never be relieved by Longmuir before their
arrival in our midst. Even if I had heard that he was coming the
following day, I knew that I should not have the effrontery to
depart from Karenni leaving him in such a predicament. I sent off
urgent messages to the Gurkhas to booby trap all the village huts
and rice barns throughout the area with grenades and plastic
charges and to ensure that there was in each village a team of men
who understood how these were to be armed, when they received
news that the Japanese were close to their village. Then feeling
that I had done all that I could do in the circumstances, I settled
down to wait.

It was at about this time that the doctor had his first seizure.
We were sitting around in the mess hut after supper one night, and
the conversation had inevitably turned to Indian politics. I had
been goading the doctor a little with his virulent nationalism, and
he was in the midst of a heated reply when suddenly his head went
back and a sinister gargling noise began to issue from his throat.
For a moment I wondered what on earth he was trying to do, and
then he gradually went blue in the face and collapsed.

I tried to remember just what it was that one did with people
when they had a fit. I had the vaguest of recollections that it was
necessary to get something between their teeth, and started
desperately to try to prize his mouth open with a spoon.
Fortunately I was relieved in my ministrations by a Karen who
had been a medical orderly in the hospital at Kyaukkyi before the
war and who was acting as our cook. He carried the doctor off to
his bed and when I went over to see him a few minutes later he
had regained consciousness. He was looking very exhausted and
obviously did not want to talk to me very much. So I let him lie.

Back in the mess hut I asked Sergeant Rowe what the hell it
could be. My immediate impulse was to say that it was an epileptic
fit. Rowe told me that the doctor had had a similar attack before
while Jerry had been at main headquarters, but had asserted
vigorously the following morning that it was nothing serious and
begged not to be evacuated. The prospect of having in our midst a

person liable to seizures at a time when we were expecting large enemy bodies was to say the least of it a little alarming. I knew that a Lysander would be coming in to the air strip within the next two days as Turrall had gone out to Rangoon to attend a conference and was due to return to his sub-area at any time.

In the morning I broached the subject of his evacuation to the doctor very gently. He was evidently as afraid as I was that he was an epileptic, for he kept on asserting that there was nothing wrong with him. I liked De Wanjea and had a big respect for him. He was a Congress-minded Indian from Bengal, which is not a very attractive Indian province, but he had the quality of courage in a high degree and I did not want him to come to any harm. In the end I decided that it would depress him so much to order him to go to Rangoon that I would let him stay on in the camp. I felt that it was his problem, and that he alone would pay the penalty if his health broke completely.

The following day there were reports of two hundred Japanese in Bikodo overlooking the Lipeykhi fields. I sent a message to Rangoon that it was inadvisable to send any Lysanders in to the landing strip until further notice. But that night there was a top priority message in to the effect that it was absolutely vital that Turrall should return forthwith and that an aeroplane would be arriving at ten o'clock the following day. I decided that I should like to see Turrall, partly because I had heard so very much about him and he was evidently a rather colourful character, and partly to get the picture of what was going on in the Pegu Yomas. So I set out at six o'clock the following morning after an early cup of tea in the direction of Lipeykhi, taking with me Saw Bla Baw and two mobile levies from main headquarters.

The journey to Lipeykhi was easier than the journey back because it was mostly down hill. From the main headquarters camp on Mount Plakho it took one a little less than an hour to reach the paddy field in front of Takokodo, and then one had a stiff uphill climb for two hours to reach the summit of the next range. After that there was another steep descent into Lipeykhi itself. I had been six weeks in main headquarters and was not in very good condition. It rained all the way and there appeared to be more leeches than ever once one left Mount Plakho. I was very tired as I came down the last hill above the landing strip.

Above three hundred yards from the bottom I heard an aeroplane circling in the mist. I had not had time to warn the Gurkhas to expect the Lysander that day and was afraid that there might be no one on the strip, so I broke into a shambling run, slithering and sliding down the slope in a grotesque fashion with the levies jogging along behind me. As I came out into the clearing a very heavy shower of rain obscured my visibility. I could see two or three figures at the other end of the strip laying out some pieces of squashed bamboo in the shape of a letter of the alphabet. As I moved towards them they moved out of my line of vision, and I saw that it was a Z, which in our ground to air code meant *'Do not land'*. The Lysander came in low over the strip and one of the figures in a Gurkha hat fired a red Very light.

Panting heavily, I ran on towards him. It was Pashi Taunkhul, a Naga serving in the Assam Rifles who had been one of my original parachute party. The other two were mobile levies. Pashi Taunkhul was a tall thin youth very different from the Gurkhas and he had been my orderly at one time. I could tell that he was rather on edge. Just as I was about to speak there was a most violent explosion further up the valley in the direction of the Bikodo track. Pashi Taunkhul's eyes rolled horribly, and he kept on repeating something about *'Many Japs'* and a *'Rendezvous'*. I told him to tell Havildar Bom Bahadur to withdraw to main headquarters if Lipeykhi was too hot for him, and that under no circumstances was it worth any of them getting killed. Then he set off up the valley at a jog trot.

7

The journey back across the mountain to Takokodo in the rain was very tiring. I had not eaten since the previous night and it was about two o'clock in the afternoon before we reached the village. Saw Bla Baw had sent one of the two mobile levies on ahead to ask the headman to prepare a meal. This was a very good one of buffalo meat and rice and they gave us each a bottle of rice beer with it which went a long way to revive my spirits. All the village elders squatted on their haunches around me while I ate. They had heard that the Japanese were in Bikodo and were rather worried. Their village had been badly plundered by the 72nd Independent Mixed Brigade when it had passed through, but I noticed rather to my surprise that there were still a number of chickens and black pigs grubbing for food amid the thick wooden stilts that supported the houses.

I told the headman that the Gurkhas had that morning exploded a charge in the path of the enemy, but that I had not yet received details of the encounter. My guess was that the Japanese were unlikely to go to Takokodo in any case, as the easiest routes from Lipeykhi lay south in the direction of Simudo, or north east towards Lomati and the Yunzalin Chaung. While we were talking two scouts came in from Lipeykhi with the news that the Gurkhas had had a most successful ambush on the Bikodo track earlier in the day and that the Japanese had withdrawn to Bikodo. This information was the signal for considerable rejoicing. Every one suddenly started to feel very confident, and to boast that even if the Japanese did come to the Pyagawpu valley they would receive a gigantic defeat.

Rather heartened I set off up the hill in the direction of main headquarters. But I found the going very hard and was ready for little else but bed by the time I reached the camp. The little son of Saw Digay, who had stayed on as my orderly when Jerry went away, brought me a tin full of boiling water, and I went into a kind of bell tent that we had erected out of two silk personnel parachutes and stripped down for a bath. While I was washing messengers arrived from Havildar Bom Bahadur with a written message confirming what I had learnt from the villagers in Takokodo. West of Lipeykhi there is a very precipitous path leading up into the hills in the direction of Bikodo. At one place near the foot of it it passes through a narrow ravine with sharp cliffs on either side of it. Here Havildar Bom Bahadur had laid out five hundred yards of detonating cord with subsidiary lines attached to it at thirty yard intervals, each having either a hand grenade or a plastic charge covered with rocks attached to it. He had laid a detonating device at the point where the ravine broadened out into the valley and two of the mobile levies had volunteered to shelter themselves in a nearby crevice in the ground and to explode the charge when the enemy came.

Bom Bahadur had taken up his main ambush position about one hundred and fifty yards further back covering the entrance to the ravine, where he had sited two Bren guns, a two inch mortar and an assortment of other small arms. His plan was to allow the Japanese to move forward to the entrance of the ravine and open fire as they exposed themselves across the open ground. The first burst from the Brens was to be the signal for the two Karen volunteers hiding in their hole in the ground to detonate the charge. It was hoped that by this time the ravine would be well filled by other Japanese moving up behind the leading section and that over the area of approximately five hundred yards covered by the primer cord there would be heavy casualties. The ambush appeared to have worked well. The explosion had been terrific and what Japanese had been left unhurt in the ravine had taken to their heels leaving about thirty-five of their comrades lying on the ground.

A party of Gurkhas had later gone forward to try and search the bodies for identity discs and other papers but the enemy had sited an automatic weapon further up the ravine and had fired on them as soon as they appeared.

The news gave me an appetite, and that night we broached a bottle of gin from a case that the last Lysander had brought in to Lipeykhi. Rowe did not drink. But Storrie and the doctor and I finished it off. All over the camp there was a great deal of chattering and singing and I knew that the levies were in good heart. I felt that if the Japanese withdrew from Lipeykhi without further battle, we should have achieved a great moral victory.

The whole of the following day I awaited further news, but none came. In the end I decided that no news was probably good news, and went to bed in still better heart than the previous night. There were several very lengthy high priority messages on the evening schedule about when and where the Sittang breakout would occur, but I was far too concerned with what the next information from Bikodo would be to concentrate upon them. At that time it was about three days short of the full moon, and movement at night was a possibility to be contended with.

Another dawn came and with it renewed anxiety. I finally decided that that day I would hear that the Japanese had withdrawn from Bikodo. On the strength of this I settled down after breakfast to find my way through the latest news relating to the Sittang break-out prospects, and to draft a precis of it to be relayed to all the other sub-stations. The main concentration was in the Pegu Yomas opposite Kyaukkyi and in the captured operation order it was shown that they were to rendezvous in the foothills just south-east of the town, very close to where Turrall's headquarters was. The Rangoon headquarters were very worried about Saw Torry's position in the plains in the direct line of advance of the enemy breaking out. They wanted him to withdraw his men to the hills where there would be better scope for manoeuvre. I drafted a message to him instructing him to do so and another to the Colonel trying to explain the set up as concisely as possible. It appeared that Shwegyin was no longer occupied by our own troops.

Just as I was finishing my messages two mobile levies from Lipeykhi arrived, looking very wet and depressed. I could tell from the excited conversation that was going on around me in Karen that there had been grave developments. They had a message from Bom Bahadur. The Japanese had moved into Lipeykhi from several directions in very great strength at dawn and the villagers had fled south. The Gurkhas had been taken completely by surprise and had had to withdraw into the jungle in the direction of Takokodo. Bom Bahadur reported that he would take up ambush positions astride the tracks crossing the mountain from Lipeykhi to Takokodo that night, and move back to Mount Plakho in the morning. I settled down with a mug of tea and a pipe and worked out an appreciation of the situation in the orthodox Army style and at the end of it was no nearer to knowing what to do.

In the evening Saw Thet Wa arrived in camp and I took him along to my hut and gave him a stiff glass of gin. All this had come as a great blow to him after the excitement of making his farewells and moving down to the air strip to await evacuation, and he was looking very drawn and tired. I asked him what he thought about the situation. He had lived and worked with the Japanese and knew far more about them than I did. I told him that to begin with I had believed that this large organised force was moving down to the Sittang River from the Mawchi road to line the river bank and provide a reception for their comrades escaping from the Pegu Yomas. But now they had moved away from the river bank and Neville, Turrall and Saw Torry were once more in charge of that area. It seemed most unlikely that, if their only object was to withdraw, they would choose a route through the centre of the mountains in the height of the monsoon. The only conclusion that I could come to was that this was an organised drive against the guerillas in my area.

Saw Thet Wa agreed with me. The Japanese were reported to be well-equipped and in aggressive mood and were taking tactical precautions. That being decided, it remained to consider what measures we could take against them. The Gurkhas with the mobile levies in the Lipeykhi area were the only effective force that I had with which to harass a party of this size. But they had already fought one battle and would not be in very good shape when they arrived on Mount Plakho the following day. It seemed to me that an air strike was the best answer. In that season the betting was very much against fast fighter planes ever finding their target, but I nevertheless checked on the map the areas that Saw Thet Wa knew to be occupied by the enemy and drafted a top priority message to Rangoon asking for them to be straffed.

Later when I had gone to bed everything seemed to come much

clearer in my mind. These Japanese were either on their way out
to Siam or else they were on an organised anti-guerilla drive. If the
former was the case they would be certain either to move north
from Lipeykhi along the easy route to Lomati and the Yunzalin,
or else south to Simudo. But in no circumstances would they cross
the high range between Lipeykhi and Takokodo. On the other
hand, if their next move was in the direction of Takokodo, it
seemed almost certain that they were coming specially to clean up
the guerilla areas around Lipeykhi and Pyagawpu. I decided that if
the enemy occupied Takokodo I should have to move main
headquarters to some temporary hiding place in the jungle.

I sent for Saw Thet Wa again soon after daylight and told him
about my plans for a move. The question arose as to where we
should go. To decide this the *thugyi* and Saw San Sen were
brought into the discussion. The prospect of our leaving the area
depressed the *thugyi* considerably as he said that all the villagers
relied upon us to defend them. I tried to explain to him that there
were many valuable and secret documents in the headquarters and
that it was imperative that these should not fall into enemy hands
and that there were not enough of us to repel an enemy attack.
But it was very difficult to make him understand. His world very
naturally centred on his village and for the enemy to seize and
destroy that was to him the worst thing that could possibly
happen.

Saw Thet Wa, however, was capable of a wider outlook, and
appreciated the situation. After a good deal of argument in Karen
language he at last made the headman understand the necessity of
preparing an alternative position. Saw San Sen was not argument-
ative. It was not his village anyway and he did not mind where we
went. I unrolled a map on the table and we started to look for
possible hide-outs in the event of the enemy making a sweep
through the area. After a good deal of discussion it was decided
that the best places to withdraw to were either in the dense jungle
country to the east on the banks of the Yunzalin or in similar
country just north of the Thelaw Klo and east of the Pyagawpu
police station. This being agreed upon I sent parties of mobile
levies off to both areas to build huts. In the monsoon it was quite

impossible to bivouac at random in the forest.

I then went into a long conference with Sergeant Rowe about just what wireless equipment we should have to take with us. We were working a great many schedules daily at the time, and the charging of batteries presented difficulties. Most of this was done by means of a petrol generator, which was unfortunately a rather weighty object to carry round in the jungle. There was however a little hand generator which was sufficient to keep a wireless on the air for one schedule a day. In the end I decided to take this alone. It would at any rate be sufficient to keep us in contact with our headquarters and I hoped that the batteries would last without recharging until the Japanese had moved further on. As it was the amount of equipment that it appeared necessary to take with us was enormous.

The Gurkhas came in about midday. They were tired and wet and very depressed. An atmosphere of defeat hung about the camp. Finding no rum left in the store, I gave Havildar Bom Bahadur a couple of bottles of gin that were lying on one side. Gurkhas are very conservative in their tastes, and he looked a bit dubious at trying what he considered to be a sahib's drink. But I explained to him that it was only another harmless variant of the rice spirit that his people were accustomed to drink, and he thanked me and went back to his men.

About an hour later Corporal Storrie came rushing into my hut with a look of amused bewilderment on his face. I looked out of the doorway in the direction in which he pointed, and there was the indomitable Man Bahadur sitting nicely relaxed in the entrance to a hut with his boots off. He was solemnly filling an empty glass to the brim with gin. Having done this, he regarded it quizzically, took a tentative sniff and then, throwing back his head, drank it at a single draught. I expected to see him choke, but when he lowered his glass he seemed completely unmoved. Catching my eye, he called across that it was a very good drink.

By four o'clock there were still no signs of the enemy moving in our direction, and I almost came round to thinking that their next move would now be north-east. Scouts from Takokodo reported that the villages of Bikodo, Balawkhi and Lipeykhi were swarming with Japs and that mules and horses accompanied the party. This last item seemed to be slightly sinister, as it was the first report of Japs with animal transport that I had ever had in Cerise sub-area.

Just before nightfall there was the distant sound of automatic fire to the north. The local villagers reckoned that it was from the Tibawkhi area, which seemed to suggest that the enemy was indeed moving north. I slept an uneasy night, and in the morning was awakened with the news that it was Timukhi, not Tibawkhi, where the firing had occurred the previous night. This brought the war right back again onto our own doorstep. At midday there were short sharp bursts of light automatic fire from the valley below and a little later Saw Thet Wa came running up with the news that large numbers of enemy had moved into Takokodo from all sides and had spread out across the paddy fields to the foot of Mount Plakho.

I gave orders for the petrol generator and all the spare wireless equipment to be taken to a secret cave nearby. I also bundled most of the files and stationery into a sack and sent that off to hiding. We had the maps of the whole of Hyena area pinned together on the walls of my hut with the positions of all the guerilla posts marked upon them, and these were also taken down. Rations were at the time very short, but I ordered what remained, which amounted to sufficient to keep the whole party going for just over two days, to be divided among the men. Then we paraded in the rain and I made a little speech which must have sounded very ineffective, explaining that we were going to move the headquarters down to the Thelaw Klo as it was quite impossible to allow the wireless and office to fall into enemy hands.

I sent the doctor and Storrie on ahead with an elephant load of wireless equipment to the new camp and instructions to open upon the first schedule the following day. The rest of us did not leave until the late afternoon. The mountain was swathed in mist and it was raining harder than ever. Long before dark I realised that we should never reach the new camp in daylight. So when we finally came to an obscure little mountain valley containing several paddy huts, I gave the order to halt for the night. Sergeant Rowe, who was an indifferent marcher, had dropped a little behind, and did not come in until a quarter of an hour later. His feet were very sore, and he was cursing horribly. Padu was with him. One of Padu's knees invariably gave way when it came to walking, but he was chuckling merrily at the general discomfiture all the same.

We all crowded into the paddy huts, sprawling down as best we could across the floor. I felt an awful sense of defeat, wondering whether I had done right to move the headquarters. The prospects of maintaining full wireless communication with all our out-stations for more than two days on the batteries that we had with us sustained by a single handgenerator were bad, and that seemed to be the only justification for the move. On the other hand, if there was indeed an anti-guerilla drive going as I suspected, the chances of the levies putting up any effective resistance were slight.

Taking off my boots I found that my socks were soaked in blood, and I removed no less than seven partially filled leeches from my ankles. I ate an American K Ration and then settled down to smoke the cigarettes inside it. Much to my surprise the levies were chattering away quite merrily around me. After the monotonous existence in the mist on Mount Plakho the novelty of the situation had doubtless intrigued them. We all had to sleep at very close quarters on the floor, and the night was made hideous by great grinding snores from every direction. Sinking further and further into a slough of despondency I also must have slept.

At dawn we moved on and, reaching the new camp an hour later, found Storrie and the doctor with breakfast ready for us and in wireless communication with Rangoon. It was a very pleasant clean camp at a much lower altitude than the one on Mount Plakho. The atmosphere was not so damp and it was good to escape from the mist. The first message that came in informed us that six RAF Thunderbolts had attempted an air strike on Lipeykhi the previous day, but had been unable to find the target. There was also a very corrupt situation report suggesting that the break-out was starting in the Sittang Valley. While I was smoking my pipe after breakfast and talking to the doctor we both thought we heard a continuous rumbling sound in the distance. I was quite certain that it was not thunder as the noise was much too regular. When I asked the Karens they agreed with me.

'The break-out's starting at last,' I said to the doctor.

The previous day Saw Thet Wa and Havildar Bom Bahadur had remained on Plakho with a small rearguard, and instructions to join us if the Japanese started to move up onto the hill towards the camp. About eleven o'clock I received a message from Saw Thet Wa that the Japanese were moving south towards Pyagawpu down the valley. He was quite certain that they were now unlikely to discover the old main headquarters camp and was anxious that we should return to it. After forty-eight hours of alarums and excursions I felt little desire for another move, and decided to remain in the new camp for the following night at any rate before returning. But it was necessary for one of the wireless operators to return to open up on the early morning schedule to Rangoon.

Much to everyone's surprise Sergeant Rowe volunteered to go on condition that a Karen was found to carry his pack. In headquarters the British personnel had been used to having their packs carried by the villagers when on the move, and he preferred to walk back that night with nothing on his shoulders to making the journey fully laden the following day. After he had gone Storrie, the doctor and I spent a pleasant evening round the fire listening to the rain beating against the roof of our hut and drinking rice spirit.

When we reached Mount Plakho the following day we learned that the Japanese had indeed started their long awaited break-out from the Pegu Yomas. About 17,000 of them had been skulking in those low malarious hills since the beginning of the monsoon under conditions which would have caused any other army on earth to surrender. When the time came they followed the instructions contained in the captured operation order to the letter. No attempt was made to fight. Each Japanese soldier was carrying two short bamboo poles to get him across the Sittang River and very little else. A great many of them were almost naked and without arms. Thus equipped they started to cross the tarmac Toungoo—Pegu road in a steady stream and make straight for the river bank as fast as they could.

The slaughter was terrific. British, Indian and Gurkha troops were strongly entrenched along the road and railway line and patrols of tanks and armoured cars moved in between the various posts. Heavy concentrations of artillery were firing almost continually day and night. On the river bank fighter aircraft kept up an almost continuous daylight patrol. Personally I dislike the Japanese so intensely that I cannot stand within a dozen yards of one of them without a cold chill running down my spine. But I cannot but admire them in the break-out. They may be cruel and brutal, arrogant in victory and treacherous in defeat. But when their time came, they certainly knew how to die. Out of the 17,000 that set out for the Sittang River bank from the Pegu Yomas only 4,000 ever reached the east bank. There were over four hundred prisoners taken, probably more than had ever been taken previously in the whole of the Burma campaign. And the remainder died on the way. As an example of military stupidity it must rival the Charge of the Light Brigade and in the same way it has an epic quality.

The next three weeks passed as in a dream. All the first day the Japanese party from Lipeykhi were crossing the Thelaw Klo at Pyagawpu and heading south along the Bilin Chaung. Scouts of mine who were watching the track saw more than a thousand pass. A very few stragglers had fallen beside the track as the force moved, and these were despatched by the levies during the next few days. All the time we could hear the guns rumbling away in the Sittang Valley and a steady flow of situation reports started to come across the wireless.

The general opinion appeared to be that the Japanese breaking out in the direction of Kyaukkyi would head south along the river bank in the direction of Shwegyin. This was confirmed during the next few days when we learned that the Karen guerillas south of that town were fighting a terrific battle on the banks of the Shwegyin Chaung.

I decided that Saw Torry and Sergeant Moore were almost certain to be overrun in their exposed position at Kywethalin in the centre of the paddy country south of Kyaukkyi. But in actual fact in the ensuing battle theirs was the most successful sub-area of all. Catching the enemy just after they had crossed the river and when they were in a completely exhausted condition and had had no chance to proceed to their prearranged rendezvous and reform, they inflicted great slaughter. A wireless had been dropped to Sergeant Moore a few days before and he was at last in contact with main headquarters. Each day he seemed to be able to report a bigger bag of Japanese casualties than the day before. For a while they were almost out of ammunition, but fighter aircraft succeeded in keeping them supplied whenever the situation grew desperate.

Turrall was flown into the Lipeykhi airstrip two days after we returned to main headquarters. Barron, who had originally been down with Saw Torry in Kywethalin but had been evacuated wounded early in the operation also came in on the same plane and walked over to join me at main headquarters for a few days before Colonel Howell ordered him south to the area of the Bilin Chaung to Saw Tannay's area. Turrall himself went straight on over to his old camp in the foothills above Kyaukkyi. A few days later I received a message from him to the effect that two thousand Japanese troops with mules and horses were passing down the road from Kyaukkyi to Shwegyin and that his ambush parties had been chased a considerable distance into the hills. Then he went off the air. To the north of him Neville's area was to begin with very quiet.

East of the Yunzalin Chaung there were no longer any Japs moving south down the main track from the Mawchi road to Papun. Otter area reported that large numbers were now for the first time crossing the Salween River into Siam at Kemapyu on rafts. Colonel Howell announced his intention to return to main headquarters, but in the meantime a suggestion was put forward to move certain guerilla parties across the Salween into the Karen areas of Siam. For this purpose two officer reinforcements, Christopher Leng and Paddy McCoul, were flown in by Lysander.

The Lipeykhi landing strip had deteriorated badly during the monsoon. After heavy rain the surface was like glass, and when Castledine landed with Leng and McCoul he was unable to pull up in the necessary distance and his Lysander went careering into the jungle at the far end of the field and turned up on its nose. Fortunately no one was hurt, but the plane was unable to make the return journey. Castledine had been flying throughout the monsoon and was really badly in need of a rest. His immediate reaction to his accident was to declare the landing strip unfit for further use, and I therefore sent him a message telling him to come over to Mount Plakho to look at another piece of ground in the vicinity which I thought might conceivably serve.

While he was over at main headquarters, however, the weather improved and on a dry day Squadron Leader Turner, who commanded the Lysander flight that was working with us, arrived unheralded and made a perfect landing on the Lipeykhi strip. He was rather annoyed that Castledine was not waiting there to be taken back, but much to our joy he declared that the strip was still practicable on a dry day.

A few days later he came in again bringing two RAF fitters who repaired Castledine's Lysander, which he was able to fly out in due course.

Paddy McCoul and Christopher Leng, the new arrivals, were charming quiet-spoken tall young men. Paddy had been in Greece in the resistance. Earlier in the year he had been dropped into a battalion of the Burmese puppet army working for the Japanese in the Mokpalin area south of the Karen hills after it had expressed itself ready to come over to the British side. At that time the situation had been very fluid and there had been plans to push a regular brigade across the Sittang at Mokpalin and down to Moulmein, but these had been later abandoned. For a while Paddy's operation had gone very well. They had taken some airdrops and laid ambushes on the coast road. There had been comparatively few Japanese in the area and each day Paddy had expected to hear that the regular troops were approaching. Gradually, however, almost imperceptibly, the morale of the Burma Defence Army men had begun to collapse. One day they received a report that the Japanese were sending troops into their area to clean up the guerillas. A week had passed during which Paddy had been very wary, and then just as he was regaining confidence he had awakened one morning to find that all the Burmese had fled during the night. A few minutes later he saw Japanese converging on his camp from all directions. He and the other Britishers had run for their lives leaving most of their equipment behind them.

For a while they hid around in the nearby hills, having signalled

Rangoon for instructions. The whole area was swarming with Japanese and these were even seen to be bringing up typewriters into their camps which was taken as evidence that they intended to stay. Rangoon suggested that Paddy should stay on in an intelligence role, but by this time he had firmly decided that, as the man on the spot, he was the person best qualified to say what was possible and what was not, and he ordered his party to make its way north to an air strip that Mongoose area was operating. Paddy's account of his adventures sounded amusing in retrospect, but they must have been hair-raising as they occurred.

8

During the next week Leng, McCoul and I sat around in the Mount Plakho camp awaiting further instructions. The trend of the Japanese movements was definitely in a southerly direction along the river bank apart from occasional foraging expeditions into the foothills, and peace had descended once more on the Pyagawpu valley. But in the north a party of several hundred Japanese break-out troops under the General Koba had broken across the river, and it was believed that they might move south through my sub-area.

Daily I expected news of my relief, but none came. I did not learn until later that Jock Longmuir had been killed in an encounter with enemy stragglers on his way into Otter area to relieve George Scurfield's party.

During that time we did not often listen to the news on the wireless, and we had not heard of the atomic bomb. Then one morning Sergeant Rowe came into my hut before breakfast with the information that the Japanese Government was asking for peace terms. Frankly I decided that his ears must have deceived him, but everyone else in the camp seemed very excited. During the next few days, however, a period of disillusion gradually set in, and then Paddy McCoul received orders from the Colonel to go over to Bachit's sub-area. Bachit was apparently due for leave and the Colonel himself had decided to return to Mount Plakho as no more parties appeared to be using the Kauludo—Papun track. But there were large concentrations in both Turrall's and Neville's sub-areas north of Shwegyin.

Then the day after Paddy left the news did at last come through that the war was over. All the operators started signalling greetings messages to one another in clear and our spirits rose in incredulous, almost delirious, wonder. But in actual fact it made very little immediate difference in Hyena area where the Japanese were out of wireless contact with their superior commanders. We were instructed that in future there would be no further air strikes except in dire emergency and that we were only to fight if it should be necessary in self-defence. But the Japanese on the east bank of the Sittang in no way moderated their tactics and during those next few days seemed to run completely amok in an orgy of looting, burning and killing.

Turrall was courageous enough to walk down from his camp in the foothills to the plains, accompanied only by a single Karen carrying a flag of truce in an attempt to stop the war. He was very badly beaten up and the Karen was killed before his eyes. Probably he himself would have shared the same fate, if a specially printed pamphlet in Japanese characters had not been dropped by the RAF in the area informing the Japanese commander of the Imperial Government's surrender and telling him that Turrall was the personal representative of the British Corps Commander across the river.

Organising the surrender of the Japanese army is not quite as simple as it would seem. A Japanese soldier will only take orders from his own immediate superiors. During the following days we listened anxiously to the wireless. There were reports that various Colonel-Princes from the Imperial House were proceeding to all the more distant fronts to order a cease fire. Allied envoys had landed in Japan. But always as a footnote to the news came the communique 'Heavy fighting continues all along the Burma front'. One resented intensely the prospect of getting killed after the armistice.

Then Colonel Howell arrived in main headquarters and the same day there came a message from Rangoon to the effect that I was at last to be relieved by another V Force called Maginn who was to be flown in to Lipeykhi the following morning. To the north there was still no information of the approach of General Koba's force, but Colonel Howell felt that before I was evacuated I should spend a few days showing Maginn round the countryside and laying on some ambushes facing north. I was by this time tired of it all, and had no thought but to be repatriated to England on the first available ship, so that it was in a particularly sullen frame of mind that I set out for Lipeykhi.

It rained throughout the journey and when I reached the village about twelve o'clock there was no news of the arrival of the aeroplane. For a moment my spirits revived when I saw how pleased the Gurkhas and the villagers were to see me after my long absence on Mount Plakho. The schoolmaster informed me in his halting English that, although all their pigs and poultry had been slaughtered by the enemy, they had succeeded in purchasing a goat with which to give me a farewell party.

In the afternoon we at last heard a plane circling in the mist above and I set off from the village to walk down to the landing strip across the paddy fields with Havildar Bom Bahadur. When I arrived there was no sign of an aeroplane or of any of the sentries, but a Karen arrived shortly afterwards with the information that the Lysander had crashed on the hillside.

That day Peter Arkell's plane had been rather more heavily loaded than usual. Coming in to land he had misjudged his distances and realising that he was about to touch down half way up the strip had attempted to regain height. As he strove desperately for altitude a sinister green mountainside approached him at alarming speed. For several agonising seconds he battled to clear it, and then at the very summit his Lysander crashed into the undergrowth and turned over. It was a complete wreck, but Maginn was unhurt and Peter Arkell himself escaped with a broken arm. When I arrived on the scene he had already been extricated from the wreckage and was smoking a cigarette while Maginn tried desperately to stop the flow of blood that was spreading down his shirt in an ugly dark stain.

I gave him some morphia and we rigged up a stretcher of bamboo on which we carried him down to the little hut beside the landing strip. He was talking quite coherently, but his arm was still bleeding and he was starting to feel the pain. I sent two runners off to the wireless on Mount Plakho asking for a Lysander with a doctor aboard to be sent to Lipeykhi the next day, and at the same time requesting that De Wanjea be sent over in case the Lysander should for any reason be held up. As ill luck would have it, De Wanjea was at that time south of the Thelaw Klo and it would take him two days to reach us.

That night Peter Arkell must have suffered hell. But he still kept up his RAF air crew veneer of careless light heartedness.

Apart from giving him tea, cigarettes and more morphia there was nothing one could do except be sympathetic. In the morning it was raining very hard and the clouds were very low over the mountains. His arm still appeared to be bleeding a little, and I decided to myself that unless he was evacuated that day he would probably die.

The headman and the schoolmaster came over about ten o'clock with the local medicine man. These herb doctors possess great prestige in the mountain villages of Karenni and lead a celibate ascetic existence dedicated to their profession. In amongst the strange mixture of animist beliefs which they apply there must be a good deal of sound practical medical knowledge. I remembered Guthrie telling me how helpful the local herb doctor had been to him when he had been lying on Mount Plakho with a broken leg in the early days of the operation. I showed this one Peter Arkell's arm and he said that he could stop the bleeding. How exactly he did it I do not know. He mumbled Arkell's name and applied a yellow lotion made out of herbs and sure enough the bleeding did stop.

After tea just when I had given up hope of a Lysander coming that day we heard an aeroplane engine overhead. It was no longer raining but there were two pools of water on the landing strip. I asked Arkell whether it would be all right to fire the green Very lights when we saw the plane and he said yes. I always went through agony when a Lysander landed on that strip. This one went careering on up into the undergrowth at the far end of the strip but was undamaged. The pilot was Squadron Leader Turner and he had with him an RAF doctor. While the doctor went over to look at Arkell we manhandled the Lysander out of the undergrowth and turned it round so that it was facing down the strip. It had been another very close shave. Turner had realised that the landing strip was in a dangerous condition, but decided to crash land if necessary in case Arkell was in a really bad way.

Meanwhile Maginn, the doctor and some Gurkhas brought Arkell over to the plane. The meeting between Arkell and Turner amused me immensely as I felt it was very typical of the RAF's approach to life. Arkell was very weak, but he told the Squadron Leader about his crash.

'It was one of my better crashes,' he ended up, grinning.

'It was one of my better planes,' replied Turner.

It was by that time about five o'clock, and the Lysander took off with just sufficient time to spare in which to make Rangoon before darkness.

Epilogue

I myself was evacuated from Karenni about a fortnight later. Like most things that happen to one in the services it was something of an anti-climax. There was no further fighting in Cerise sub-area after Arkell went, and there was time for the inevitable period of boredom to set in. When I left Lipeykhi the villagers had a fresh crop of paddy coming up in the fields and just enough rice to see them through till the harvest time. All their livestock had been destroyed and most of their clothes and bedding burnt, but when we made our farewells the headman and the schoolmaster and old Saw Jo Po assured me that they would be all right. They looked disappointed when they heard that I was going back to England, and made me promise that if I ever returned to Burma I would get in touch with them. I felt that from thenceforth I was an honorary citizen of Lipeykhi. But I knew in my heart, and I think that they knew in theirs, that we should never meet again.

Back in Rangoon there was more delay and anti-climax. The prisoners of war were being evacuated from Malaya and Siam and my repatriation was postponed for over a month. I hitchhiked up the road to the ancient Burmese city of Pegu where I found Jerry Hayter and his headquarters established in a pleasant shady mansion of teak. The remains of V Force were going up to Kengtung on the Chinese border and I lived with them in Pegu until they went. Then I went down to wait in the transit camp in Rangoon until my turn came to go home.

All around me the urgency that one had felt during the war years was falling off. People were already starting to jockey for position in the peace, and in the process to lose that sense of unity with all mankind that they had had when they were living dangerously. I felt a great relief at having at last escaped from the kind of existence in which one could only think ahead from day to day. But in its place there was a strange emptiness all around me.

As I lazed in the sun on the deck of the troopship as it steamed through the Red Sea, I felt that I was returning to a world that I did not properly understand.